Introduction

This workbook is designed to be used in conjunction with *Edexcel GCSE Maths – Higher Tier Revision and Classroom Companion*, published by Letts and Lonsdale. As such, it is suitable for use by students following either the linear (2540 and 1380) or modular (2544 and 2381) specifications.

The worksheets are matched page for page to the revision and classroom companion, and consist of structured questions with spaces for answers, plus extension questions. They feature interesting and challenging exam-style questions, which are designed to reinforce understanding of the material that is covered in the specifications.

To help students following the modular courses, the contents page includes details of the unit(s) that each page of questions is relevant to.

An answer book for the questions in this workbook is also available.

Please note, a separate workbook is available for Foundation Tier students.

Consultant Editor: John Proctor

A respected Education Consultant with over 14 years teaching experience, John Proctor is an expert in mathematics and ICT education. He is the former Director of Specialist College, St. Mary's Catholic School in Astley.

Contributor: Tina Foster

Formerly the Head of Mathematics at a large comprehensive school, Tina Foster is now employed as a Mathematics Consultant by a local authority and has an excellent understanding of the new two-tier specification, which she is helping to implement in local schools.

Contents

If you are following one of the modular specifications, the numbers in brackets indicate which unit(s) the content of each page is relevant to.

Place Value

1 Complete the following table. The first row has been done for you.

Place Value of Digits					Number
10 000 Ten Thousands	**1000** Thousands	**100** Hundreds	**10** Tens	**1** Units	
		3	2	6	Three hundred and twenty six
a)	5	3	0	7	....
b) 7	3	1	5	8	....
c)		....	....		Five hundred and sixty
d)	1	....	....	7	.... , two hundred and forty ....
e)	....	....	....	....	Fourteen thousand and fifty two

2 Round 493 507 to the nearest...

a) 10 000 .... **b)** 1000 .... **c)** 100 .... **d)** 10 ....

3 Round 109 109 to the nearest...

a) 10 000 .... **b)** 1000 .... **c)** 100 .... **d)** 10 ....

4 If the attendance at a football match was 32 000 to the nearest thousand, what is the lowest possible number and the highest possible number of people that could have attended the match?

Lowest possible number: .... Highest possible number: ....

5 The number of boys who attended school on a particular day was 440 to the nearest ten. On the same day the number of girls who attended school was 460 to the nearest ten.

a) What is the lowest possible difference between the number of boys and the number of girls who attended school on that day? ....

....

b) What is the highest possible difference between the number of boys and the number of girls who attended school on that day? ....

....

6 Draw a table to show the place value of each digit in the following numbers:
  a) one   **b)** eighty seven   **c)** four hundred and nine
  d) six thousand, two hundred and twenty three   **e)** fifty thousand and five

7 Round 30 715 to the nearest...
  a) thousand   **b)** hundred   **c)** ten

Rounding Numbers

1 Round...

a) 7.321 to...   **i)** 1 decimal place ....   **ii)** 2 decimal places ....

b) 16.781 to...   **i)** 1 decimal place ....   **ii)** 2 decimal places ....

c) 0.01765 to...   **i)** 2 decimal places ....   **ii)** 3 decimal places ....

d) 0.1053 to...   **i)** 1 decimal place ....   **ii)** 3 decimal places ....

e) 7.0707 to...   **i)** 1 decimal place ....   **ii)** 2 decimal places ....

2 Dave weighs 68.4kg to 1 decimal place. What is the lowest measurement and the highest measurement possible for his actual weight to 2 decimal places?

Lowest possible weight: ....   Highest possible weight: ....

3 Helen's height is 1.65m to 2 decimal places. What is the lowest measurement and the highest measurement possible for her actual height to 3 decimal places?

Lowest possible height: ....   Highest possible height: ....

4 Round...

a) 432 to...   **i)** 1 significant figure ....   **ii)** 2 significant figures ....

b) 9154 to...   **i)** 1 significant figure ....   **ii)** 2 significant figures ....

c) 10 047 to...   **i)** 2 significant figures ....   **ii)** 4 significant figures ....

d) 0.0238 to...   **i)** 1 significant figure ....   **ii)** 2 significant figures ....

e) 0.0001736 to...   **i)** 2 significant figures ....   **ii)** 3 significant figures ....

f) 0.010366 to...   **i)** 2 significant figures ....   **ii)** 3 significant figures ....

5 The attendance at a pop concert was 5700 to 2 significant figures. What is the difference between the lowest possible actual attendance and the highest possible actual attendance?

....

....

....

---

6 Round 135.6742 to **a)** 1 decimal place **b)** 2 decimal places **c)** 1 significant figure
d) 2 significant figures **e)** 3 significant figures

7 Round 0.06038 to **a)** 1 decimal place **b)** 2 decimal places **c)** 3 decimal places
d) 1 significant figure **e)** 2 significant figures **f)** 3 significant figures

8 Fran's weight to 1 decimal place is 47.6kg. What is the difference between her highest possible weight and her lowest possible weight to 2 decimal places?

9 **a)** Use your calculator to work out the value of $(1.46)^2 \times 6.71$. Write down all the digits on your display.
b) Round your answer to a suitable degree of accuracy.

Numbers 1

1 Solve the following without using a calculator. Show all your working.

a)
```
    475
+    28
_____
```

b)
```
  23179
+  4830
_____
```

c)
```
    238
-    99
_____
```

d)
```
  43008
-  1559
_____
```

e)
```
    423
x    36
_____
```

f)
```
   4705
x    91
_____
```

g)
```
16 ⟌ 608
```

h)
```
13 ⟌ 3341
```

i) 41 x 100

j) 573 x 1000

k) 423 ÷ 10

l) 8 ÷ 1000

2 a) A whole number is multiplied by 1000 to give an answer of 234 000

What is the number? ....

b) A whole number is divided by 100 to give an answer of 0.08.

What is the number? ....

3 a) The number 864 900 is divided by a power of 10 to give the answer 8.649.

What is the power of 10 used?

....

b) The number 763 is multiplied by a power of 10 to give the answer 76 300 000.

What is the power of 10 used?

....

4 Solve the following without using a calculator. Show all your working.

a) 3001 + 999   b) 4735 + 381 + 49   c) 4079 - 497   d) 13 574 - 9281   e) 473 x 67   f) 375 x 413

g) 4037 ÷ 11   h) 47 748 ÷ 23   i) 940 x 10   j) 403 x 100   k) 11 x 1000   l) 33 942 x 10 000

m) 408 ÷ 10   n) 55 ÷ 100   o) 6 ÷ 100   p) 33 942 ÷ 10 000

5 A whole number is multiplied by a power of 10 giving an answer of 23 000. When the whole number is divided by the same power of 10 the answer is 2.3 a) What is the whole number?

b) What is the power of 10?

Numbers 2 & 3

1 **Here are eight numbers:**

(3) (4) (6) (7) (11) (15) (20) (21)

a) Which three numbers are even numbers? ....

b) Which two numbers are factors of 40? ....

c) Which two numbers are factors of 45? ....

d) Which four numbers are factors of 42? ....

e) Which two numbers are multiples of 7? ....

f) Which three numbers are multiples of 2? ....

g) Which three numbers are prime numbers? ....

h) Which number has an odd number of factors? ....

2 **Here are ten numbers:**

(5) (8) (11) (19) (22) (24) (31) (36) (47) (81)

a) Which six numbers are odd numbers? ....

b) Which three numbers are factors of 72? ....

c) Which three numbers are factors of 110? ....

d) Which three numbers are multiples of 3? ....

e) Which three numbers are multiples of 4? ....

f) Which five numbers are prime numbers? ....

g) Which two numbers have an odd number of factors? ....

3 **What is the reciprocal of...**

a) 8? .... **b)** 25? .... **c)** 0.5? .... **d)** $\frac{3}{4}$? ....

4 **The reciprocal of a number is 0.1**

What is the number? ....

5 **Express the following numbers in prime factor form:**

a) 36 .... **b)** 64 .... **c)** 930 ....

Numbers 2 & 3 (cont)

6 a) What is the highest common

factor of 20 and 36?

....

....

....

....

b) What is the lowest common

multiple of 20 and 36?

....

....

....

....

7 a) What is the highest common factor

of 64 and 100?

....

....

....

....

....

b) What is the lowest common multiple

of 64 and 100?

....

....

....

....

....

8 What is a) the highest common factor and **b)** the lowest common multiple of 6, 15 and 24?

....

....

....

....

....

9 a) The highest common factor of two numbers is 4. The lowest common multiple of the same two

numbers is 60. What are the two numbers?

....

....

b) The highest common factor of three numbers is 15. The lowest common multiple of the same three

numbers is 90. What are the three numbers?

....

....

---

10 Here are ten numbers:

9, 14, 25, 29, 41, 50, 61, 70, 84, 100

a) Which three numbers are **i)** factors of 200, **ii)** multiples of 25, **iii)** multiples of 7, **iv)** prime numbers?
b) Which of the above numbers has the reciprocal 0.02?

11 What is the reciprocal of a) 100, **b)** $\frac{1}{100}$, **c)** 0.01, **d)** $\frac{99}{100}$?

12 Express the following numbers in prime factor form: **a)** 30, **b)** 100, **c)** 2048

13 What is the highest common factor and lowest common multiple of...
a) 15 and 18, **b)** 40 and 58, **c)** 15, 18 and 24?

Integers 1 & 2

1 **a)** Put the following integers into ascending order (lowest to highest):

14, -3, -1, 5, 12, -7, -11, 2

....

b) Put the following integers into descending order (highest to lowest):

-230, 467, 165, -62, -162, 70, -320, 8

....

2 Complete the following calculations:

a) **i)** $1 - 3 + $ ☐ $= 6$ **ii)** $6 + $ ☐ $= 2$ **iii)** $-6 + $ ☐ $= -11$

iv) $-4 - $ ☐ $= -9$ **v)** $4 - $ ☐ $= -4$ **vi)** $-3 - $ ☐ $= 5$

vii) $-6 \times $ ☐ $= 12$ **viii)** $5 \times $ ☐ $= -20$ **ix)** $-6 \times $ ☐ $= 6$

x) $-12 \div $ ☐ $= -2$ **xi)** $36 \div $ ☐ $= -9$ **xii)** $-45 \div $ ☐ $= 9$

b) **i)** $-4 - 6 + $ ☐ $= 2$ **ii)** $6 - $ ☐ $- 3 = 11$ **iii)** $-8 - 3 - $ ☐ $= 5$

iv) ☐ $+ 2 - 5 = -9$ **v)** $14 - 1 + $ ☐ $= -15$ **vi)** $4 - 11 + $ ☐ $= -5$

c) **i)** $\dfrac{-6 + \boxed{}}{-3} = 7$ **ii)** $\dfrac{-6 + 2 - \boxed{}}{-5} = 4$ **iii)** $\dfrac{\boxed{} - 6 - 3}{-1} = 4$

iv) $\dfrac{-3 \times -5 \times \boxed{}}{-6} = 10$ **v)** $\dfrac{9 \times \boxed{} \times -2}{4 - 6} = 9$

d) **i)** ☐ $+$ ☐ $= -4$ **ii)** ☐ $-$ ☐ $= -3$ **iii)** ☐ $\times$ ☐ $= -18$

iv) ☐ $\div$ ☐ $= -10$ **v)** ☐ $\times -5 \times$ ☐ $= 30$

3 Complete the following calculations by inserting = and −, +, x or ÷ into the correct boxes:

a) 6 ☐ 9 ☐ -3 **b)** 2 ☐ 3 ☐ -7 ☐ 12

c) 9 ☐ 1 ☐ -3 ☐ -3 **d)** -50 ☐ 10 ☐ 5 ☐ 0

e) 6 ☐ -3 ☐ 10 ☐ 19 ☐ 1

f) 10 ☐ -2 ☐ 6 ☐ 2 ☐ 0

Integers 1 & 2 (cont)

4 The following table shows the highest temperatures (in °C) for eight places on a particular day:

Place	Athens	Berlin	Cairo	Cardiff	London	Madrid	Moscow	New York
Temperature	15	-2	25	2	6	13	-6	18

a) What is the difference in temperature between the following places:

i) Athens and Berlin?..

ii) Cairo and Moscow?..

iii) Berlin and Moscow?..

b) The following day the temperature in Cardiff had fallen by 2°C and the temperature in Moscow had fallen by 5°C. What was the new difference in temperature between Cardiff and Moscow?

....

5 Below is part of a bank statement:

LONSDALE BUILDING SOCIETY

Date	Description	Deposit	Withdrawal	Balance
11/12/03				£226.30
12/12/03	The Toy Shop		-£49.99	£176.31
13/12/03	Gas Bill		-£21.03	£155.28
13/12/03	Cheque	£25.00		£180.28
16/12/03	La Trattoria		-£32.98	[ ]
19/12/03	Rent		[ ]	-£112.70

a) What was the balance on 16/12/03 after the withdrawal of £32.98?

....

b) On 19/12/03 there was a withdrawal to pay for rent. How much was the withdrawal?

....

6 Put the following integers into ascending order:

3, -3, -11, 0, 4, 19, -36, 74, -1, 100

7 Complete the following:

a) $6 - 8 =$ b) $-4 - 4 =$ c) $-1 - 1 + 2 =$ d) $-5 \times -6 \times 10 =$ e) $-5 \times 3 \times 6 =$ f) $-15 \div 3 \times -4 =$ g) $100 \div 4 \times -1 =$

8 Complete the following calculations:

a) $\boxed{} - 3 = 12$ b) $-8 - \boxed{} = 3$ c) $-6 + \boxed{} - 2 = 11$ d) $-14 + 20 + \boxed{} = -10$ e) $\boxed{} + 4 - 8 = -15$

Upper & Lower Bounds

1 a) Some ribbon is measured as 7.4cm to the nearest mm. What are the upper and lower bounds of the length of the ribbon?

....

b) Kevin cut off 3.2cm of ribbon. Find the greatest and shortest length of ribbon left.

....

....

2 The weight of a BMW car is given as 1900kg to the nearest 100kg. Find the difference between the greatest and least possible weight of this car as a percentage of the given weight.

....

....

3 Ellie measured the length and width of the cover of a book, her measurements are accurate to 1 decimal place.

a) What is the greatest possible length of the

cover of the book? ....

b) Find the shortest possible length. ....

c) Between what bounds must the width of the cover lie?

....

18.8cm

24.6cm

4 A floor is measured as 3.8m x 4.9m to the nearest 10cm.

a) Calculate the largest possible area of floor.

....

b) Calculate the smallest possible area of floor.

....

3.8m

4.9m

c) As an inequality, write down the range of possible values for the actual area of floor.

....

d) Calculate the upper and lower bounds of the perimeter of the floor.

....

5 Julie measures the length and width of a sheet of A4 paper, the dimensions are given opposite. She then cuts out a circle of radius 7cm. All measurements are to the nearest cm. Find **a)** the greatest possible area of paper left **b)** the least possible area of paper left.

30cm

21cm

6 A car travels at an average speed of 37.6 miles per hour over a distance of 53.2 miles. Both measurements are correct to 1 d.p. Calculate the range of possible values for the time taken.

Estimating & Checking

1 **a)** **i)** Without using a calculator estimate the answer to 106 x 53

....

    ii) Work out the actual answer using a calculator ....

  b) **i)** Without using a calculator estimate the answer to 3.8 x 15.2

....

    ii) Work out the actual answer using a calculator ....

  c) **i)** Without using a calculator estimate the answer to $\dfrac{29.4 \times 5.8}{19.6}$

....

    ii) Work out the actual answer using a calculator ....

  d) **i)** Without using a calculator estimate the answer to 384 726 x 0.00071

....

    ii) Work out the actual answer using a calculator ....

2 **John and Donna collect and keep all their loose change. The table below shows how much they collected for three successive months.**

MONTH	JOHN	DONNA
JUNE	£7.36	£9.10
JULY	£8.90	£16.58
AUGUST	£13.47	£4.52

a) John has calculated that he has collected £29.73 altogether.

  i) Check by estimation whether this is likely to be correct.

....

  ii) Check John's calculation for accuracy.

....

b) Donna has calculated that she has collected £31.20 altogether.

  i) Check by estimation whether she is likely to be correct.

....

  ii) Check Donna's calculation for accuracy.

....

....

3 **Check the following calculations by estimation and then for accuracy. Make any necessary corrections.**
    a) 13 + 29 + 43 = 82 **b)** 9.06 + 11.58 + 7.23 + 13.86 = 41.73
    c) (3 x 6.25) + 92 − 10 = 101.75 **d)** (4.7 x 6.3) + (0.8 x 9.5) = 40.21

Order of Operations

1 **Calculate the following:**

a) $7 + 5 \times 2$

....

....

b) $14 \times 5 - 3$

....

....

c) $6^2 + 4 \times 2$

....

....

d) $\dfrac{15}{3} + 6$

....

....

e) $18 \times 2 - 5^2$

....

....

f) $\dfrac{30}{6} - \dfrac{40}{10}$

....

....

g) $2^3 + 4^3 \times 3$

....

....

h) $6 \times 7 - 10 \times 3 + 8$

....

....

i) $15 - 3 \times 6 \times 2 + 5$

....

....

2 **a)** Put brackets in the following expression so that its value is 43:

$13 - 3 \times 4 + 3$

b) Put brackets in the following expression so that its value is -8:

$13 - 3 \times 4 + 3$

c) Put brackets in the following expression so that its value is 70:

$13 - 3 \times 4 + 3$

d) Put brackets in the following expression so that its value is 4:

$13 - 3 \times 4 + 3$

e) Put brackets in the following expression so that its value is 20.5:

$3 \times 1.4 + 4 \times 2.5$

f) Put brackets in the following expression so that its value is 12.12:

$7 + 3.2 \times 6 - 4.4$

---

3 **Calculate the following:**

   a) $4 + 3 \times 13$ **b)** $4 \times 3 - 13$ **c)** $4 - 3 \times 13$ **d)** $4^2 \div 2 + 3$ **e)** $9 + 15 \div 5$ **f)** $4 + 7 \times 3 - 15$
   g) $14 \div 4 - 5$ **h)** $3 + 7 - 5 \times 3^2$

4 **Put brackets in the following expression so that its value is...** **a)** -1   **b)** 35   **c)** -51

   $3^2 - 4 \times 5 + 10$

5 **Put brackets in the following expression so that its value is...** **a)** 54   **b)** -2   **c)** 6

   $4^2 - 3 \times 4 + 2$

Powers 1 & 2

1 **Work out the value of...**

a) 2^3 ....
b) 3^2 ....
c) 4^3 ....

d) 10^3 ....
e) 3^4 ....
f) 1^5 ....

2 **Here are ten numbers:**

10   18   25   27   45   64   80   125   133   196

a) Which three numbers are square numbers? ....

b) Which three numbers are cube numbers? ....

c) Which one of these numbers is a square number and a cube number? ....

d) Which of the above numbers is equal to $10^2 - 6^2$? ....

e) Which of the above numbers is equal to $4^3 + 2^4$? ....

3 **Work out the value of...**

a) $(-3)^2$ ....
b) $(-3)^3$ ....
c) $(-5)^2$ ....

d) $(-5)^3$ ....
e) $(-1)^2$ ....
f) $(-1)^3$ ....

4 **Find the value of...**

a) $2^3 \times 2^2$ ....
b) $3^2 \times 3^1$ ....

c) $4^3 \times 4^2 \times 4^1$ ....
d) $2^3 \div 2^2$ ....

e) $10^4 \div 10^2$ ....
f) $6^4 \div 6^0$ ....

g) $(2^2)^2$ ....
h) $(4^3)^2$ ....

i) $(10^2)^3$ ....
j) $(2^2 \times 2^3)^2$ ....

k) $\dfrac{10^2 - 6^2}{4^3}$ ....
l) $\dfrac{4^3 + 2^6}{8^2}$ ....

m) $\dfrac{(4^1)^3}{8^2}$ ....
n) $\dfrac{2^2 \times 2^1 \times 2^4}{4^3}$ ....

5 **Work out the value of...**

a) $27^{\frac{2}{3}}$ ....
b) $64^{\frac{2}{3}}$ ....
c) $16^{\frac{3}{4}}$ ....

d) $100\,000^{\frac{4}{5}}$ ....
e) $1024^{\frac{2}{5}}$ ....
f) $1^{\frac{9}{10}}$ ....

6 **Work out the value of...**

a) 4^4 b) 4^1 c) $4^4 \times 4^1$ d) $4^3 \times 5^2$ e) $8^0 + 3^3$ f) $6^2 - 3^2$ g) $\dfrac{8^2}{2^5}$ h) $\dfrac{3^3 - 7^1}{2^2}$ i) $\dfrac{10^2 + 3^3 + 5^0}{8^2}$

7 a) What is $3^3 \times 9^2$ as a single power of 3?   b) What is $5^2 - 3^2$ as a single power of 2?

c) What is $8^2 \times 2^4$ as a single power of 4?

Roots

1 **Work out the value of...**

a) $\sqrt{25}$ ....

b) $36^{\frac{1}{2}}$ ....

c) $\sqrt{144}$ ....

d) $196^{\frac{1}{2}}$ ....

e) $64^{\frac{1}{3}}$ ....

f) $\sqrt[3]{1}$ ....

g) $8^{\frac{1}{3}}$ ....

h) $\sqrt[3]{1000}$ ....

i) $27^{\frac{1}{3}}$ ....

2 **Here are ten numbers:**

 2 4 5 8 10 20 27 36 64 80

a) Which three numbers have an integer square root? ....

b) Which three numbers have an integer cube root? ....

c) Which one of these numbers has an integer square root and an integer cube root? ....

d) Which of these numbers is equal to $\sqrt{144} - 8^{\frac{1}{3}}$? ....

e) Which of these numbers is equal to $81^{\frac{1}{2}} \times \sqrt{16}$? ....

3 **Work out the value of...**

a) $(\sqrt{4})^2$ ....

b) $(\sqrt[3]{8})^2$ ....

c) $\sqrt{4^2 \times 25}$ ....

d) $100^{\frac{1}{2}} \times \sqrt[3]{27}$ ....

e) $64^{\frac{1}{2}} \times \sqrt[3]{64}$ ....

f) $16^{\frac{3}{2}}$ ....

4 **a)** What is $\sqrt{4} \times 8$ as a single power of 4? ....

b) What is $\sqrt[3]{27} \times 3$ as a single power of 3? ....

c) What is $\sqrt[3]{64} \times 16^{\frac{1}{2}}$ as a single power of 2? ....

d) What is $\sqrt{9} \times 1^3 \times \sqrt{144}$ as a single power of 6? ....

5 **Simplify the following surds:**

a) $\sqrt{27}$ ....

b) $\sqrt{50}$ ....

c) $\sqrt{54}$ ....

d) $\sqrt{90}$ ....

e) $\dfrac{\sqrt{15}}{\sqrt{3}}$ ....

f) $(5 - \sqrt{7})^2$ ....

6 **a)** Rationalise the denominator of $\dfrac{4}{\sqrt{7}}$

b) Rationalise the denominator of $\dfrac{5}{\sqrt{11}}$

7 **Work out the value of...**
a) $169^{\frac{1}{2}}$ **b)** $\sqrt[3]{125}$ **c)** $\sqrt{81}$ **d)** $125^{\frac{1}{3}}$ **e)** $225^{\frac{1}{2}}$

8 **Find the value of...**
a) $(\sqrt{9})^3$ **b)** $(\sqrt[3]{8})^2$ **c)** $\sqrt[3]{6^2 + 28}$ **d)** $4^{\frac{3}{2}}$ **e)** $64^{\frac{2}{3}}$

9 **Simplify the following surds:**
a) $\sqrt{200}$ **b)** $\sqrt{80}$ **c)** $\sqrt{63}$

Standard Index Form

1 **Write the following examples of standard form as ordinary numbers:**

a) 2.3×10^2 ....

b) 2.3×10^3 ....

c) 4.21×10^4 ....

d) 6.32×10^1 ....

e) 7.467×10^3 ....

f) 3×10^{-2} ....

g) 2.3×10^{-3} ....

h) 4.21×10^{-4} ....

i) 6.324×10^{-2} ....

2 **Write the following numbers in standard form:**

a) 600 ....

b) 473 ....

c) 42 000 ....

d) 413 256 ....

e) 496.3 ....

f) 0.032 ....

g) 0.47 ....

h) 0.000631 ....

i) 0.1 ....

3 The number of seconds in one year is approximately 3.1×10^7. Use this number to calculate...

a) How many seconds are there in 5 years? Give your answer in standard form.

b) On her next birthday Chloe has calculated that she will be 4.34×10^8 seconds old!
How old will Chloe be in years?

c) How many seconds are there from Chloe's next birthday to her 21st birthday.
Give your answer in standard form?

4 **Calculate the following. Give your answers in standard form.**

a) $9.23 \times 10^2 + 4.71 \times 10^3$ ....

b) $7.15 \times 10^5 - 9.68 \times 10^4$ ....

c) $2.34 \times 10^4 \times 3.6 \times 10^7$ ....

d) $5.5 \times 10^7 \div 1.1 \times 10^9$ ....

5 In 1901 the population of England and Wales was 3.26×10^7. If the area of England and Wales is 151 000km^2 (to the nearest thousand), calculate what the population per square kilometre was in 1901. Give your answer to 2 significant figures.

6 In one minute light will travel a distance of approximately 1.8×10^{10} metres.
a) How far will light travel in 1 hour? Give your answer in standard form. b) How far will light travel in 1 year? Give your answer in standard form. c) The Sun is approximately 1.44×10^{11} metres away. How long does it take light to travel from the Sun to the Earth? d) A light year is the distance travelled by light in one Earth year. Our nearest star, after the Sun, is 4.3 light years away. How far away is this star in metres? Give your answer in standard form.

Fractions 1

1 Here are eight fractions:

$$\frac{35}{50} , \frac{16}{40} , \frac{60}{90} , \frac{28}{40} , \frac{30}{40} , \frac{40}{100} , \frac{84}{120} , \frac{10}{25}$$

a) Which three fractions are equivalent to $\frac{2}{5}$? ....

b) Which three fractions are equivalent to $\frac{7}{10}$? ....

2 Express the following fractions in their simplest form:

a) $\frac{27}{30}$ ....

b) $\frac{42}{6}$ ....

c) $\frac{84}{105}$ ....

d) $\frac{108}{184}$ ....

3 **a)** Arrange the following fractions in ascending (lowest to highest) order:

$$\frac{5}{6} , \frac{3}{5} , \frac{11}{15} , \frac{2}{3} , \frac{1}{2}$$

....

b) Arrange the following fractions in descending (highest to lowest) order:

$$\frac{9}{40} , \frac{3}{5} , \frac{5}{8} , \frac{9}{10} , \frac{1}{4}$$

....

4 Write down two fractions that are greater than $\frac{7}{10}$ but less than $\frac{5}{6}$.

....

5 **a)** Write the following improper fractions as mixed numbers:

i) $\frac{11}{5}$ .... **ii)** $\frac{13}{6}$ .... **iii)** $\frac{24}{5}$ .... **iv)** $\frac{32}{3}$ ....

b) Write the following mixed numbers as improper fractions:

i) $3\frac{1}{3}$ .... **ii)** $5\frac{1}{4}$ .... **iii)** $11\frac{3}{5}$ .... **iv)** $20\frac{1}{20}$ ....

6 Write down three fractions that are equivalent to each of the following:

a) $\frac{2}{3}$ **b)** $\frac{4}{7}$ **c)** $\frac{9}{11}$

7 Express the following fractions in their simplest form and then arrange then into ascending order:

$$\frac{28}{35} , \frac{38}{40} , \frac{75}{100} , \frac{42}{84} , \frac{99}{110}$$

8 Write down three fractions that are greater than $\frac{4}{5}$ but less than $\frac{9}{10}$.

Fractions 2

1 Solve the following additions and subtractions without using a calculator. Show all your working and give your answers in their simplest form.

a) $\frac{3}{4} + \frac{2}{3}$

b) $\frac{2}{9} + \frac{7}{8}$

c) $4\frac{1}{2} + 2\frac{9}{10}$

d) $7\frac{5}{8} + 4\frac{1}{3}$

e) $\frac{9}{10} - \frac{1}{2}$

f) $\frac{13}{15} - \frac{2}{3}$

g) $4\frac{4}{5} - 1\frac{3}{8}$

h) $9\frac{1}{6} - 4\frac{3}{5}$

2 At a football match $\frac{5}{12}$ of the crowd are over 40 years old, $\frac{1}{4}$ of the crowd are between 20 years old and 40 years old, and the remainder of the crowd are less than 20 years old.

What fraction of the crowd are less than 20 years old? Give your answer in its simplest form.

....

....

....

....

....

3 Solve the following multiplications and divisions without using a calculator. Show all your working again and give your answers in their simplest form.

a) $\frac{1}{4} \times \frac{2}{5}$

b) $\frac{9}{10} \times \frac{2}{7}$

c) $\frac{3}{4} \div \frac{9}{10}$

d) $\frac{7}{8} \div \frac{7}{12}$

e) $3\frac{1}{2} \times 1\frac{3}{5}$

f) $3\frac{1}{4} \times 1\frac{5}{7}$

g) $4\frac{1}{2} \div 2\frac{2}{3}$

h) $1\frac{1}{2} \div 2\frac{1}{4}$

i) $\frac{8}{9} \times 4$

j) $\frac{7}{10} \div 3$

4 Solve the following without using a calculator. Show all your working.

a) $\frac{7}{10} + \frac{5}{8}$ b) $2\frac{1}{3} + 4\frac{3}{8}$ c) $\frac{9}{10} - \frac{2}{3}$ d) $4\frac{1}{2} - 3\frac{7}{10}$ e) $\frac{2}{5} \times \frac{7}{10}$ f) $\frac{13}{15} \div \frac{4}{5}$

g) $3\frac{1}{4} \times 1\frac{2}{3}$ h) $4\frac{1}{5} \div 3\frac{1}{2}$ i) $4\frac{1}{2} \times 5$ j) $2\frac{1}{3} \div 6$

Calculations Involving Fractions

1 James wants to buy a CD player that costs £240.

As a deposit he pays $\frac{1}{8}$ of the cost. How much deposit did James pay?

....

....

2 Mary buys a new car that costs £13 000.

As a deposit she pays $\frac{2}{5}$ of the cost. The remainder she pays monthly over a period of 4 years.

a) How much deposit does Mary pay?

....

....

b) What is her monthly repayment?

....

....

c) At the end of the 4 years Mary decides to sell her car. It is now worth £7150. Express its value now, after 4 years, as a fraction of its value when new. Give your answer in the simplest form.

....

....

3 A shop holds a sale where all items are reduced by $\frac{1}{6}$.

a) Calculate the sale price of an item which cost £93.60 before the sale.

....

....

b) The sale price of another item is £121.50. Calculate its price before it was reduced.

....

....

....

4 A football match lasts $1\frac{1}{2}$ hours. During the match, player number 9 sits on the bench for a total of 15 minutes. He is on the pitch for the rest of the time. Express the total length of time that player number 9 is on the pitch as a fraction of the time that the match lasts. Give your answer in its simplest form.

5 In a sale, a washing machine has its original price reduced by $\frac{1}{2}$. The following week the sale price is further reduced by $\frac{1}{4}$.

a) If the washing machine originally cost £600, calculate its sale price after **i)** the first reduction, **ii)** the second reduction.

b) If a washing machine in the same sale costs £150 after both reductions what was its original price?

6 Express 40 seconds as a fraction of 1 hour.

Decimals 1 & 2

1 Complete the following table (the first row has been done for you).

	Place Value of Digits							Decimal Number
	100 Hundreds	10 Tens	1 Units	DECIMAL POINT	$\frac{1}{10}$ Tenths	$\frac{1}{100}$ Hundredths	$\frac{1}{1000}$ Thousandths	
			3	•	4	2		3.42
a)	1	0	2		5			
b)		1	3		4	7	1	
c)								8.407
d)		9	0		0	3	1	
e)								423.008

2 Use a calculator to write the following fractions as either recurring or terminating decimals. If the decimal is recurring, place a dot (•) over the digit or digits that repeat continuously.

a) $\frac{2}{3}$ ....

b) $\frac{2}{5}$ ....

c) $\frac{1}{11}$ ....

d) $\frac{7}{9}$ ....

3 Arrange the following decimals in ascending order of value:

$$6.3, \ 0.36, \ 3.6, \ 0.306, \ 0.63$$

....

4 Convert the following recurring decimals into fractions:

a) 0.7777...

b) 0.6363...

5 Write the following fractions as decimals. For each recurring decimal, place a dot (·) over the digit or digits that repeat continuously.

a) $\frac{3}{8}$ b) $\frac{2}{9}$ c) $\frac{1}{30}$ d) $\frac{22}{25}$ e) $\frac{4}{15}$

6 Arrange the following decimals in descending (highest to lowest) order:

14.32, 1.432, 143.2, 13.42, 14.23, 1.342

7 Mrs Green goes shopping. She buys four tins of baked beans at 37p each, 3 tins of spaghetti at 29p each and 2 boxes of cornflakes at £1.37 each. She pays for her goods with a £10 note. How much change does she receive?

8 Convert the following recurring decimals into fractions: a) 0.1111... b) 0.4545...

Multiplication with Decimals

1 Solve the following without using a calculator. Where possible show all your working.

a) 4.7 x 10   **b)** 13.246 x 10   **c)** 0.00146 x 100   **d)** 136.3 x 1000

....

e) 7.56 x 13   **f)** 4.72 x 2.3

g) 16.56 x 17.3   **h)** 4.713 x 1.56

2 If **27 x 36 = 972** write down, without making any further calculations, the value of...

a) 2.7 x 36 ....   **b)** 27 x 0.36 ....   **c)** 2.7 x 3.6 ....

d) 0.027 x 36 ....   **e)** 0.27 x 0.36 ....

3 If **231 x 847 = 195 657** write down, without making any further calculations, the value of...

a) 0.231 x 847 ....   **b)** 231 x 84 700 ....

c) 0.231 x 847 000 ....   **d)** 2310 x 8.47 ....

---

4 Solve the following without using a calculator.
Where possible show all your working.
a) 15.67 x 10   **b)** 0.0101 x 100   **c)** 3.4671 x 1000   **d)** 2.32 x 11
e) 4.67 x 1.8   **f)** 146.2 x 2.45   **g)** 13.33 x 0.23   **h)** 9.4 x 0.003

5 If **3.52 x 4.7 = 16.544** write down, without making any further
calculations, the value of...
a) 352 x 47   **b)** 3.52 x 47   **c)** 0.352 x 4.7   **d)** 3.52 x 0.047

6 A school holds a raffle. The three prizes cost £24.65, £17.99
and £9.89. 130 tickets were sold at £1.25 each.
How much profit did the school make from the raffle?

7 Jim is going to hire a cement mixer. The cost is £24.50 for the
first day and £3.75 for each extra day. Jim wants to hire it for 7
days. How much will it cost him in total?

8 A shirt costs £24.95. How much is this in euros if £1 = €1.6?

£24.95

Division with Decimals

1 Solve the following without using a calculator. Where possible show all your working.

a) 16.3 ÷ 10

b) 0.347 ÷ 10

c) 14 632.4 ÷ 100

d) 1.2467 ÷ 1000

....

e) 37.6 ÷ 8

f) 41.04 ÷ 1.2

g) 1141.72 ÷ 0.23

h) 549.6 ÷ 1.2

2 If 72.8 ÷ 56 = 1.3 write down, without making any further calculations, the value of...

a) 72.8 ÷ 5.6 ....

b) 7.28 ÷ 56 ....

c) 72.8 ÷ 0.56 ....

d) 0.728 ÷ 56 ....

e) 728 ÷ 56 ....

3 If 27 x 34 = 918 write down, without making any further calculations, the value of...

a) 918 ÷ 27 ....

b) 918 ÷ 3.4 ....

c) 91.8 ÷ 27 ....

d) 9.18 ÷ 3.4 ....

e) 91.8 ÷ 340 ....

4 Solve the following without using a calculator. Where possible show all your working.
a) 7.162 ÷ 10 **b)** 0.0034 ÷ 100 **c)** 473.1 ÷ 1000 **d)** 707.4 ÷ 9 **e)** 24.64 ÷ 1.4 **f)** 0.08788 ÷ 0.0013

5 If 58.82 ÷ 3.4 = 17.3 write down, without making any further calculations, the value of...
a) 58.82 ÷ 0.34 **b)** 5882 ÷ 0.34 **c)** 58.82 ÷ 17.3 **d)** 3.4 x 17.3

6 A school holds a raffle. The three prizes cost £9.49, £14.99 and £19.99. Tickets cost 75p each.
What is the minimum number of tickets that need to be sold for the school to make a profit?

7 Jean is going to hire a wallpaper stripper. The cost is £8.50 for the first day and £1.25 for each extra day.
When she returns the wallpaper stripper the total hire charge is £24.75. For how many days did she hire the
wallpaper stripper?

Percentages 1

1 Calculate the following amounts:

a) 20% of 60p

b) 30% of 6.5km

....

....

....

....

2 Express...

a) £18 as a percentage of £90

b) 42cm as a percentage of 8.4m

....

....

....

....

3 Alan has kept a record of his height and weight from when he was age 10 and age 16.

Age 10	1.2m tall	40kg weight
Age 16	1.74m tall	64kg weight

a) i) Calculate the increase in his height from age 10 to age 16 ....

ii) Express this increase as a percentage of his height at age 10.

....

....

b) i) Calculate the increase in his weight from age 10 to age 16 ....

ii) Express this increase as a percentage of his weight at age 10.

....

....

4 A train ticket costs £17.60 when bought on the day of travel. If the same ticket is bought in advance it costs £15.40. Express the saving you make when you buy the ticket in advance as a percentage of the full ticket price when bought on the day of travel.

....

....

....

5 Calculate the following amounts:
a) 45% of £2.60, **b)** 80% of 6.4kg, **c)** 5% of £10.40.

6 **a)** Express 46cm as a percentage of 69cm, **b)** Express 200m as a percentage of 200km,
c) Express 550g as a percentage of 2kg.

7 A tin of tomato soup weighs 420g. Special tins weigh 546g. Calculate the increase in the weight of a special tin as a percentage of the weight of a normal tin.

8 A brand new car bought in the UK costs £18 000. The same car bought abroad costs £14 850. Calculate the decrease in the price when the car is bought abroad as a percentage of its price in the UK.

Percentages 2

1 A brand new car costs £15 000. It is estimated that it will decrease in value by 23% in the first year. What is the estimated value of the car at the end of the first year?

....

....

2 The average attendance at a football club over a season was 32 500. In the next season there was a 6% increase in the average attendance. What was the average attendance for that season?

....

....

3 Mr and Mrs Smith bought a house for £120 000. Each year since the value of the property has increased by 10%.

a) Calculate the value of the house 2 years after they bought it.

....

....

....

b) The value of the house after two years can be found by multiplying the original cost by a single number. What is this number as a decimal?

....

4 Jim buys a new motorbike for £10 000.

a) If the value of the motorbike decreases by 20% each year, calculate the value of the motorbike after three years.

....

....

....

....

b) The value of Jim's bike after three years can be found by multiplying the original cost by a single number. What is this number as a decimal?

....

5 An electrical shop has a sale. All items are reduced by 20%. The following week the shop takes 10% off its sale prices. Pat wants to buy a fridge that was priced at £100 before the sale. She reckons that she will save 30% of this price and that the fridge will now cost her £70. Is she correct? Explain why.

6 Bob weighs 120kg on January 1. Over the first six months of the year his weight increases by 5%. Over the next six months his weight decreases by 10%.
a) What is his weight at the end of the year?
b) Bob's weight at the end of the year can be found by multiplying his weight on January 1 by a single number. What is this number as a decimal?

Percentages 3

1 Phil has been told by his mum that he needs to spend 1 hour a day doing his homework, an increase of 50%. How long did Phil originally spend doing his homework each day?

....

....

....

2 An electrical shop has a sale. All items are reduced by 15%. A tumble drier has a sale price of £122.40. What was the price of the tumble drier before the sale?

....

....

....

3 A man buys an antique clock. He later sells it for £5040, an increase of 12% on the price he paid for it. How much did the clock cost him?

....

....

....

....

4 Dave is a long distance lorry driver. On Tuesday he drives 253km. This is a 15% increase on the distance he drove the previous day. How far did he drive on Monday?

....

....

....

5 Jean has her house valued. It is worth £84 000. This is a 40% increase on the price she originally paid for it. How much did Jean pay for her house?

....

....

....

6 A clothes shop has a sale. All prices are reduced by 30%. The sale price of a dress is £86.80. What was the original price of the dress?

7 Mrs Smith buys some shares. In twelve months their value has increased by 15% to £3680. How much did she pay for the shares?

8 Mr Jones collects stamps. After two years he has increased the number of stamps in his collection by 120% to 660. How many stamps did he have in his collection two years ago?

 Revision Guide Reference: Page 27

Converting Between Systems

1 Complete the following table. The first row has been done for you.

	Fraction (simplest form)	Decimal	Percentage
	$\frac{1}{2}$	0.5	50%
a)	$\frac{3}{10}$		
b)		0.45	
c)			37.5%
d)	$\frac{2}{3}$		
e)		0.125	
f)			84%
g)	$1\frac{4}{5}$		
h)		4.6	
i)			225%

2 $\frac{3}{5}$ of the CDs in Peter's collection are pop music. Is this more or less than 55% of his collection?

Explain your answer.

....

....

3 **a)** Write the following fractions and percentages as decimals:

i) $\frac{2}{5}$ .... **ii)** 35% .... **iii)** $\frac{1}{3}$ .... **iv)** 44% ....

b) Write these numbers in ascending order.

$$44\%, \quad \frac{2}{5}, \quad 35\%, \quad 0.42, \quad \frac{1}{3}, \quad 0.25$$

....

....

4 **a)** Write the following as decimals: **i)** $\frac{4}{5}$ **ii)** 90% **iii)** $\frac{17}{20}$ **iv)** 85%

b) Write these numbers in descending order: $\frac{19}{20}$, 0.75, 90%, 0.92, $\frac{4}{5}$, 85%

5 **a)** Write the following as percentages: **i)** 0.62 **ii)** $\frac{3}{5}$ **iii)** 0.56 **iv)** $\frac{29}{50}$

b) Write the following numbers in ascending order: 61%, $\frac{3}{5}$, 0.56, 0.62, $\frac{29}{50}$, 65%

Everyday Maths 1 & 2

1 **a)** Alma buys a washing machine. The price is £380 + VAT at 17.5%.

How much does the washing machine cost in total?

....

....

b) The total cost of a home stereo system is £517 including VAT at 17.5%.

What is the price of the home stereo system before VAT?

....

....

2 **Mr Smith wants to invest £20 000 for two years. He has two options:**

SIMPLE INTEREST AT 5% OR COMPOUND INTEREST AT 4.8%

a) Which option will make him the most money? Show all your working.

....

....

....

b) Which option will make him the most money after five years?
Show all your working.

....

....

....

....

....

....

....

....

3 **Peter wants to buy a car. There are two payment options:**

Cash price £8000 or 30% deposit + 24 monthly payments of £255

a) What is the deposit required for hire purchase?

....

b) Calculate the percentage increase if Peter pays for the car by hire purchase compared to buying the

car at the cash price.

....

....

....

Everyday Maths 1 & 2 (cont)

4 Mr Spark receives an electricity bill. Complete the bill by filling in the gaps.

Meter Reading				Amount (£)
Present	Previous	Units Used	Pence per unit	
32467	30277	**i)**	8p	**ii)** ....
			Quarterly charge	9.60
		Total charged this quarter excluding VAT		**iii)** ....
		VAT at 5%		**iv)** ....
		Total payable		**v)** ....

5 Use the timetable alongside to answer the following questions:

a) Grace wants to arrive in London before midday. What is the latest train she can catch from Milford station to get there in time and how long will her train journey take?

....

....

b) Simon needs to get to Woking by 11.15am because he has a job interview. What is the time of the last train he can catch from Farncombe?

....

c) What percentage of trains departing from Woking station take less than 30 minutes to arrive at London Waterloo?

....

....

Petersfield, Milford, Farncombe, Woking to London Waterloo

Mondays to Fridays

	AN	NW	AN	AN	AN
Petersfield	0752	0811	0833	0901	0928
Liphook	—	—	—	—	—
Haslemere	—	—	—	—	—
Witley	—	—	—	—	—
Milford (Surrey)	0806	0829	0845	0917	0941
Godalming	—	—	—	—	—
Farncombe	0822	0850	0900	0937	0959
Guildford	—	—	—	—	—
Reading	—	—	—	—	—
Woking	0830	0900	0907	0947	1007
Heathrow Airport (T1)	—	—	—	—	—
Clapham Junction	—	—	—	—	—
London Waterloo	0903	0932	0939	1018	1036

Mondays to Fridays

	AN	NW	AN	AN	AN
Petersfield	0949	0956	1019	1049	1055
Liphook	—	—	—	—	—
Haslemere	—	—	—	—	—
Witley	—	—	—	—	—
Milford (Surrey)	1002	1011	1032	1102	1114
Godalming	—	—	—	—	—
Farncombe	1017	1032	1047	1117	1132
Guildford	—	—	—	—	—
Reading	—	—	—	—	—
Woking	1026	1043	1059	1128	1142
Heathrow Airport (T1)	—	—	—	—	—
Clapham Junction	—	—	—	—	—
London Waterloo	1052	1111	1125	1155	1211

6 What is the total cost of a vacuum cleaner if the price is £180 + VAT at 17.5%?

7 Mr Walker wants to invest £20 000 for 3 years. He can either invest it at 6% simple interest or 5.5% compound interest. Which option will make him the most money? Show all your working.

8 Mr Brum wants to buy a car costing £6000. He buys it on hire purchase paying £124 a month for 3 years. His total repayment is £6264. What percentage deposit did he pay?

9 Mr Plug receives an electricity bill. The cost per unit is 8p and the quarterly charge is £9.60. It says on his bill that the total payable for this quarter excluding VAT is £80.24. How many units has he used this quarter?

10 Using the timetable above, what is the difference between the average journey time of Peak time trains and the average journey time of Off Peak trains travelling from Petersfield to London Waterloo? Trains that arrive at London Waterloo after 10am are classified as Off Peak.

Ratio & Proportion 1 & 2

1 **Jim weighs 70kg. His sister Cathy weighs 35kg.**

a) Calculate the ratio of Jim's weight to Cathy's weight.

....

b) Express your answer to part a) in the form 1:n ....

2 **Freya is 90cm tall. Her brother Tom is 1.35m tall.**

a) Calculate the ratio of Freya's height to Tom's height.

....

b) Express your answer to part a) in the form 1:n ....

3 $\frac{3}{7}$ **of the teachers at a school are male.** **a)** What is the ratio of male teachers to female teachers?

....

b) Express your answer to part a) in the form 1:n ....

4 **A large tin of baked beans costs 36p and weighs 450g. A small tin of baked beans costs 22p and weighs 250g.**

a) Calculate the ratio of the weight of the two tins ....

b) Calculate the ratio of the cost of the two tins..

c) Which tin represents the best value for money? Explain your choice.

....

....

5 **a)** Divide 80p in the ratio of 2:3

b) Divide 6.3m in the ratio 2:3:4

6 **£5000 is shared between three women in the ratio of their ages. Their combined age is 120 years. If Susan gets £2500, Janet gets £1500 and Polly gets the remainder, what are their ages?**

Ratio & Proportion 1 & 2 (cont)

7 In a maths class there are 30 pupils on the register and the ratio of girls to boys is 3:2. If 4 girls and 2 boys are absent from the class what does the ratio of girls to boys become?

....

....

....

....

....

....

8 A builder makes concrete by mixing cement, gravel, sand and water in the ratio 2:8:5:3 by weight. How many kilograms of sand, to the nearest kg, does he need to make 10 000kg of concrete?

....

....

....

....

....

....

9 **Opposite is a recipe for making 10 biscuits.**

a) Calculate the amount of each ingredient needed to make 25 biscuits.

....

....

....

....

b) How many biscuits can be made using 0.715kg of oatmeal?

....

....

....

....

Recipe
90g of flour

130g oatmeal

80g margarine

---

10 **100ml of semi skimmed milk contains 4.8g carbohydrate and 1.8g fat.**
 a) What is the ratio of carbohydrate to fat? **b)** Express your answer to part a) in the form 1:n

11 **A large tub of margarine weighs 500g and costs £1.10. A small tub of margarine which normally weighs 250g has an extra 10% free and costs 52p. Which tub of margarine represents the best value for money? Explain.**

12 **Divide...**
 a) 4.2cm in the ratio 1:2, **b)** 980g in the ratio 2:3:4:5

13 **450 tickets were sold for a raffle at 20p each. The ratio of the cost of prizes to profit made is 5:13. How much profit did the raffle make?**

14 **The angles of a quadrilateral are in the ratio 2:3:5:8. What is the size of the largest angle?**

15 **A large packet of washing powder weighs 2.5kg and costs £5.60. How much should a 750g packet of washing powder cost if it represents the same value as the large packet?**

1 y is directly proportional to x^2 and y = 16 when x = 8.

a) What is the value of y when x = 12?

b) What is the value of x when y = 100?

2 y is inversely proportional to x^2 and y = 4 when x = 3.

a) What is the value of y when x = 6?

b) What is the value of x when y = 12?
Leave your answer in surd form.

3 The volume, V, of a sphere is directly proportional to the cube of its radius, r. If a sphere has a volume of 33.6cm³ when its radius is 2cm, calculate the radius of a sphere of volume 14.175cm³.

4 The pressure, P, exerted by a constant force is inversely proportional to the area, A, over which the force acts. If the pressure exerted is 15N/cm² when the area is 12cm², calculate the pressure exerted when the area is 9cm².

5 a is directly proportional to bc and a = 120 when b = 6 and c = 4
a) Calculate the value of a when b = 10 and c = 6
b) Calculate the value of b when a = 66 and c = 1.2

6 m is inversely proportional to the cube of n and m = 20 when n = 0.8
a) Calculate the value of m when n = 1.6
b) Calculate the value of n when m = 20 000

Exponential Growth & Decay

① **A bacteria culture began with 4000 bacteria. Each hour the number of bacteria increased by 10%.**

a) Complete the table below.

Time, t (hours)	0	1	2	3	4	5
Number of Bacteria, N	4000					

b) Draw the graph of Number of Bacteria against Time for the first 5 hours.

c) Use your graph to estimate the number of bacteria after $2\frac{1}{2}$ hours.

....

d) What formula shows the relationship between number of bacteria and time?

....

② **The formula V = 8000 x 0.7^t gives the value of a car after t years.**

a) What is the value of the car when new?

....

b) What is the value of the car after 2 years?

....

c) Complete the table for the value of the car between 0 and 10 years.

Give the value to the nearest whole number.

Time	0	1	2	3	4	5	6	7	8	9	10
Value	8000										

d) Draw the graph of V against t.

e) Estimate how long it takes for this car to halve in value. ....

③ **Gnomes R Cool make 25 000 garden gnomes each year. The company wants to increase production by an extra 5% year on year.**
a) What is the relationship between the number of gnomes produced, N, and time, t, in years?
b) Draw a graph of number of gnomes produced against time for up to 5 years.
c) After how many complete years will Gnomes R Cool make 35 000 garden gnomes in a year?

④ **A rival company currently make 40 000 garden gnomes each year. Due to competition from Gnomes R Cool they plan to decrease production by 10% year on year. After how many complete years will Gnomes R Cool overtake this company in the yearly production of gnomes?**

The Basics of Algebra 1 & 2

1 Simplify...

a) $a + 2a$

b) $5x + 6x$

c) $11a - 6a$

d) $9p - 2p + 4p$

e) $2a^2 + 3a^2$

f) $10w^2 - w^2 + 2w^2$

g) $2a + 3b + 4a + 5b$

h) $7c - 8d - 9c + 10d$

i) $3a \times 2b$

j) $12pq \times 2r$

k) $4ab + 8cd - 7ab + cd + ab$

l) $-4x^2 + 6x + 7 + 3x^2 - 11x + 2$

m) $14 - 8p^2 + 11p + 2p^2 - 4p + 3$

2 **Explain why $2x + 3x = 5x$ is an example of an identity and not an equation.**

3 Simplify...

a) $a^2 \times a^3$

b) $4b^3 \times 3b$

c) $6p^4 \times 4p^6$

d) $r^6 \div r^2$

e) $12c^4 \div 3c^3$

f) $18a^2b \div 9a$

g) $15a^3b^2 \div 3ab$

h) $(2a^2b)^3$

4 Simplify...

a) $\dfrac{8ab^2}{4b}$

b) $\dfrac{16a^3b^2}{ab^2}$

c) $\dfrac{(4ab)^2}{2ab^2}$

d) $\dfrac{12bc^2 \times 3ab^2}{4abc}$

5 Simplify...
a) $12x + 6x$ **b)** $12x - 6x$ **c)** $12x \times 6x$ **d)** $12x \div 6x$ **e)** $4p^2 - 11p^2$
f) $19ab - 13bc + 2ab + 16bc$ **g)** $13ab + 4a^2b - 2ab^2 + 3a^2b - 4ab + 10ab^2$

6 Simplify...
a) $a^4 \times a^3 \times a^2$ **b)** $2x^2 \times 3x \times 5x^5$ **c)** $16x^4 \div 16x^2$ **d)** $20a^3b^2c \div 10a^2b$ **e)** $(4a^2)^3$ **f)** $(3a^2b)^4$

Substitution

1 If p = 2, q = 5 and r = -4, find the value of...

a) $2p + 3q$ ....

b) $2(p + q)$ ....

c) $2pq$ ....

d) p^2q ....

e) $pq - q^2$ ....

f) pqr ....

g) $p^3 + r^2$ ....

h) $\dfrac{4p}{r}$ ....

l) $p^2q^2 + \dfrac{r}{p}$ ....

j) $\dfrac{p}{q} + \dfrac{r}{q}$ ....

2 If $x = \frac{1}{2}$, $y = \frac{1}{3}$ and z = -2, find the value of...

a) $x + y$ ....

b) xz ....

c) xz^2 ....

d) $\dfrac{1}{x} + z$ ....

3 Find the value of...

a) $3x - 7$ when $x = -3$ ....

b) $4(x^2 - 1)$ when $x = -3$ ....

c) $4(x - 1)^2$ when $x = 5$ ....

d) $(x + 2)(x - 3)$ when $x = 6$ ....

e) $(x^2 - 5)(x + 8)$ when $x = -5$ ....

4 If e = 3, f = 8, g = -4 and h = $\frac{1}{4}$, find the value of...
a) ef **b)** fg **c)** gh **d)** $e + f + g$ **e)** $f + g + h$ **f)** $e^2 - f$ **g)** g^2h **h)** $f \div g$ **i)** $e^3 + g$ **j)** $2f \div g^2$ **k)** $\frac{1}{e} + h$ **l)** $e^2 + f + g^2$

5 Find the value of...
a) $5x^2 - 3$ when $x = -4$ **b)** $5(x - 3)$ when $x = -4$ **c)** $5x^2 - 3$ when $x = -2$ **d)** $(x + 3)(2x - 1)$ when $x = 2$
e) $(x^2 + 3)(x - 5)$ when $x = -1$

6 If $m = 3 \times 10^4$ and $n = 5 \times 10^3$, find the value of...

a) mn **b)** $m + n$ **c)** $\dfrac{mn}{m+n}$

Give your answers in standard form to 2 significant figures.

Brackets & Factorisation

1 **Expand and simplify...**

a) $4(2x + 1)$

b) $3(3r - 7)$

c) $2m(3m + 2)$

d) $2p(4 - p)$

e) $6r(r^2 - 3)$

f) $10x(4x^2 - 3x)$

g) $5(2y + 4) + 3$

h) $5x(2 - 3x) + 7x$

i) $11x(5 - 3x^2) - 9x$

j) $5(3x + 2) + 4(x - 3)$

k) $5(6x + 1) + 3(4x - 2)$

l) $5x(2x - 3) - 4(3x - 1)$

m) $(x + 2)(x + 5)$

n) $(2x + 3)(x + 4)$

o) $(3x - 2)(2x + 1)$

p) $(4x - 1)(x - 5)$

q) $(x + 3)(x - 3)$

r) $(4x - 1)^2$

2 **Factorise the following expressions:**

a) $5x + 10$

b) $4x - 8$

c) $6x + 10y$

d) $6x + 3x^2$

e) $10x^2 - 5x$

f) $6x^2y - 10xy$

g) $4p^2q^3r + 6pqr$

h) $x(3y + 2) + z(3y + 2)$

i) $x(4y + 3) + (4y + 3)^2$

3 **Expand and simplify...**
   a) $6(4x - y)$ **b)** $3x(2x + 5)$ **c)** $4x^2(2y - x)$ **d)** $6x(3 - x^2)$ **e)** $4(2x + 3) + 5(x - 7)$ **f)** $6x(2x - 3) + 4(x + 5)$
   g) $10x^2(4x + 3) - 6x(2x - 1)$ **h)** $(4x + 2)(3x + 2)$ **i)** $(5x + 6)(5x - 6)$ **j)** $(4x^2 + 3x)(2x + 2)$ **k)** $(2x^3 - 3)(4 - 3x^2)$

4 **Factorise the following expressions:**
   a) $9x - 15$ **b)** $9x + 9$ **c)** $20x^2 - x$ **d)** $4x - 20x^3$ **e)** $20x^2y^2 + 36xy$ **f)** $4(3x - 5) + y(3x - 5)$

5 **a)** Expand and simplify $(a + b)^2$ **b)** Without using a calculator work out the value of $8.8^2 + 2 \times 8.8 \times 1.2 + 1.2^2$

Solving Linear Equations 1 & 2

1 Solve the following equations:

a) $5x = 35$

b) $3x + 4 = 16$

c) $5x + 8 = 23$

d) $2(x + 2) = 12$

e) $5(x - 3) = 10$

f) $4(5 + 3x) = 14$

g) $\dfrac{x}{3} = 6$

h) $\dfrac{x}{2} + \dfrac{x}{6} = 10$

i) $\dfrac{x + 2}{5} = 3$

j) $5x = 2x + 9$

k) $7x = 15 - 3x$

l) $2x = x - 8$

m) $11x + 3 = 3x + 7$

n) $5 + 7x = 23 + 3x$

o) $10x - 6 = 3x + 15$

p) $8(3x - 2) = 20$

q) $5(x + 7) = 3(9 + x)$

r) $8(4x - 6) = 7(3x - 10)$

s) $\dfrac{5x + 4}{3} + \dfrac{8 - x}{2} = 10$

t) $\dfrac{9x + 10}{4} - \dfrac{4x - 4}{10} = 14$

u) $\dfrac{2x + 6}{5} = x - 3$

Solving Linear Equations 1 & 2

2 Maggie is x years old.   Nigel is twice Maggie's age.   Helen is 4 years older than Nigel.

a) Write down an expression in terms of x for their combined age.

b) Their total combined age is 64 years. Write an equation for their ages and solve it to find Helen's age.

....

....

3 ABC is a triangle:

a) Write down an expression in terms of x for the perimeter of the triangle.

....

....

b) The perimeter of triangle ABC is 50cm. Form an equation and solve it to find x.

....

....

....

4 ABCD is a rectangle:

A ────────────── B

6cm

D ◄ x cm ►◄──── 5cm ────► C

a) Write down an expression in terms of x for the area of the rectangle

....

....

b) The area of rectangle ABCD is 72cm². Form an equation and solve it to find x.

....

....

....

5 Solve the following equations to find the value of x:
a) $2x + 5 = 17$ **b)** $15 + 3x = 3$ **c)** $4x = x + 18$ **d)** $10x = 7x - 15$ **e)** $4x - 3 = 6x + 12$ **f)** $9x + 7 = 4x - 13$
g) $14 + 5x = 7x + 2$ **h)** $23 - 8x = x - 4$ **i)** $40x - 36 = 7x + 30$ **j)** $4(x + 5) = 36$ **k)** $7(2x - 3) = 14$ **l)** $6 = 4(3x - 9)$
m) $16 = 4(11 - 5x)$ **n)** $5(x + 1) = 2(x + 7)$ **o)** $11(3x + 2) = (6x - 5)$ **p)** $9(2x + 4) - 4(5x + 8) = 0$
q) $\dfrac{x - 10}{10} + \dfrac{2x + 1}{5} = 0.7$ **r)** $\dfrac{4x + 6}{2} - \dfrac{10x}{15} = 5$

6 For each of the following derive an equation and solve it to find x.

a)   **b)**   **c)**

Formulae 1 & 2

1 **Rearrange the following formulae to make x the subject:**

a) $x + 4y = 3$

b) $6x + 7y = 50$

c) $7x - 5 = 3y$

d) $\dfrac{x}{y} + 5 = z$

e) $\dfrac{x + 3y}{4} = 5$

f) $\dfrac{4x - 3}{y} = 8$

g) $5x + 3y = 3(6 - x)$

h) $4x^2 = 3y$

i) $\dfrac{x^2}{3} = 6y$

j) $5x^2 + 3 = 7y$

2 **The volume of a cone is given by the formula: Volume = $\frac{1}{3}\pi r^2 h$**

Calculate the volume of a cone in cm^3 if r = 4cm, h = 10cm and π = 3.

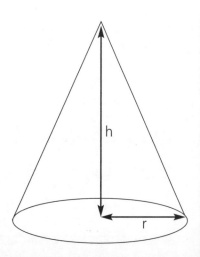

Formulae 1 & 2 (cont)

3 The distance travelled (s) by an object depends on its initial speed (u), its final speed (v) and the time of travel (t). It is given by the formula:

$$s = \left(\frac{u + v}{2}\right) t$$

Calculate the distance travelled in metres if initial speed = 4m/s, final speed = 12m/s and time = 5.5s

....

....

4 The formula that converts a temperature reading from degrees Celsius (°C) into degrees Fahrenheit (°F) is:

$$F = \frac{9}{5}C + 32$$

What is the temperature in degrees Celsius if the temperature in degrees Fahrenheit is 212°F?

....

....

....

5 The circumference of a circle is given by the formula C = 2πr, where r is the radius.
The area of a circle is given by the formula $A = \pi r^2$.

a) Write a formula for the area of a circle in terms of its circumference, C.

....

....

....

b) Use your formula to work out the area of a circle in cm^2, which has a circumference of 40cm.
Use π = 3.14 Give your answer to two significant figures.

....

6 Rearrange the following formulae to make p the subject:
a) 4p – 3 = 4q **b)** 4 – 6p = q **c)** 3(2p + 5) = 4p + 11q **d)** $3p^2 + 4 = 8q$ **e)** $\dfrac{3p^2 - 6}{4} = 2q$

7 The area of a parallelogram is given by the formula: Area = length x height. Calculate the area, in m^2, of a parallelogram that has length = 90cm and height = 1.2m.

8 The area, A, of a circle is given by the formula: $A = \pi r^2$, where r is the radius.
Calculate the radius if area = 100cm^2 and π = 3.14 Give your answer to two significant figures.

9 A garden centre buys shrubs at wholesale prices. They calculate the sale price (s), at which they are sold to customers, by increasing the wholesale price (w) by 50% and adding £2.50 per shrub.
a) Generate a formula for calculating the sale price of a shrub. **b)** If the wholesale price of a shrub is £4.00, use your formula to calculate its sale price.

Quadratic Expressions 1

1 **Factorise the following quadratic expressions:**

a) $x^2 + 6x + 8$

b) $x^2 + 7x + 10$

c) $x^2 + 9x + 6$

d) $x^2 - 9x + 20$

e) $x^2 + 9x - 10$

f) $x^2 + 8x - 20$

g) $x^2 - x - 12$

h) $x^2 - 10x - 24$

i) $x^2 - 9$

j) $x^2 - 64$

k) $x^2 - 100$

l) $x^2 - 144$

2 **Factorise the following quadratic expressions:**
a) $x^2 + 5x + 6$ **b)** $x^2 - 5x + 6$ **c)** $x^2 + 5x - 6$ **d)** $x^2 - 5x - 6$
e) $x^2 + x - 30$ **f)** $x^2 + 31x + 30$ **g)** $x^2 - 81$ **h)** $x^2 - 169$

Quadratic Expressions 2

1 Factorise the following quadratic expressions:

a) $2x^2 + 5x - 3$

b) $4x^2 + 3x - 1$

c) $2x^2 + 7x + 3$

d) $6x^2 + x - 2$

e) $6y^2 - 11y - 10$

f) $12n^2 - 11n + 2$

g) $20x^2 + 27x - 14$

h) $25x^2 - 30x + 9$

i) $49x^2 + 14x + 1$

2 Factorise the following quadratic expressions completely. You may need to rearrange them first.

a) $5a^2 + 15a - 20$

b) $12n^2 + 39n + 9$

c) $8x^2 + 2 - 8x$

d) $2x^2 + 2 + 4x$

e) $n + 3n^2 - 4$

f) $2x^2 - 3 - x$

3 Rearrange the expression $3 - 5x - 2x^2$ then factorise.

4 Rearrange the following expressions where necessary then factorise completely:
a) $42 - 34n + 4n^2$ **b)** $25y^2 + 4 - 20y$ **c)** $11x - 6x^2 - 3$

5 **a)** Factorise $7n^2 + 52n + 21$
b) Use your result from part **a)** to write 75 221 as a product of two 3-digit numbers. Explain your reasoning.
c) The number 32 207 is the product of two 3-digit numbers. What expression could you factorise to find these 3-digit numbers?

Quadratic Equations 1 & 2

1 **Factorise these quadratic equations and then solve them.**

a) $a^2 + a - 6 = 0$

b) $a^2 + 4a - 5 = 0$

c) $a^2 - 2a - 8 = 0$

d) $2a^2 - 5a - 3 = 0$

e) $3a^2 + 14a + 8 = 0$

f) $8a^2 + 6a - 9 = 0$

2 **Solve these equations, rearranging them first.**

a) $x^2 + 5x = 6$

b) $x^2 + 28 = 11x$

c) $x^2 - 3x + 3 = 1$

3 **A rectangle has dimensions as shown in the diagram opposite. The area of the rectangle is 80cm².**

$x + 2$

x

a) Write an equation for the area.

b) Solve this equation.

c) Find the perimeter of the rectangle.

4 **The squares of two consecutive whole numbers add up to 61. Let *n* be the first number.**

a) Write an expression for the second number.

b) Write an equation for the sum of the squares of the two consecutive numbers.

c) Solve the equation to find the two whole numbers.

Quadratic Equations 1 & 2 (cont)

5 Find the solutions of these equations (to 2 d.p.) by completing the square.

a) $x^2 + 10x - 4 = 0$

b) $x^2 - 10x + 1 = 0$

c) $x^2 - 4x - 3 = 0$

6 Annika's vegetable plot has dimensions as shown in the diagram. She decides to increase the size of the plot by adding x metres to the length and width.

a) Write down an expression for the area of the entire enlarged plot, multiplying out any brackets.

b) Write an expression for the area of the extension only.

c) Find x if Annika increases the area by 104m².

7 Solve these equations by either factorising or completing the square.
a) $x^2 - 7x + 3 = 0$ **b)** $4a^2 - 19a + 12 = 0$ **c)** $x^2 - x - 6 = 14$ **d)** $x^2 + 12x - 5 = 0$
e) $35 - 2a = a^2$ **f)** $4y^2 - 8y + 3 = 0$

8 The difference between the square of a number and the number itself is 72. Write down and solve an equation to find the two possible values of the number.

9 The sum of the first 'n' numbers in the sequence '1, 2, 3, 4...' is given by the formula $\frac{n}{2}$ (n + 1). How many numbers must be taken to give a sum of 55?

Quadratic Equations 3

1 Find the solutions to these quadratic equations (to 2 dp) using the quadratic formula. You may need to rearrange them first.

a) $2x^2 + 3x - 1 = 0$

b) $2 - 3x - x^2 = 0$

c) $5x^2 + 4x = 2$

2 In the triangle opposite AC is 2m shorter than AB.

a) Using Pythagoras' Theorem write down an equation for x.

b) Show how this can be simplified to $x^2 - 2x - 70 = 0$

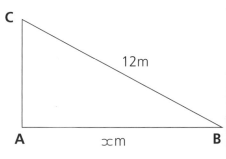

C

12m

A xm   B

c) Solve this equation using the quadratic formula.

3 Solve these equations to 1 d.p. using the quadratic formula.
  a) $x(x + 2) = 5$ **b)** $x^2 = 4x - 3$ **c)** $(x + 1)(x - 2) = 3$
  d) $x^2 + 10x - 4 = 0$ **e)** $3x^2 - 3x = 2$ **f)** $4 - 5x - x^2 = 0$

4 A square picture of side 20cm is put in a frame w cm wide.
  a) Write an expression for the area of the frame in terms of w.
  b) If the picture has an area of half the area of the frame and picture together, write an equation for w.
  c) Show that this equation can be simplified to $w^2 + 20w - 100 = 0$
  d) Solve the equation to find the width of the frame (w) to 1 d.p..

w

w   w

20cm

w

Trial & Improvement

1 The equation $x^3 - x = 15$ has a solution which lies between 2 and 3. Using trial and improvement complete the table to solve the equation and find x. Give your answer correct to 1 decimal place.

x	$x^3 - x$	Comment
2	$2^3 - 2 = 8 - 2 = 6$	Less than 15
3	$3^3 - 3 = 27 - 3 = 24$	More than 15

Answer: ....

2 The equation $x^3 + 2x = 40$ has a solution which lies between 3 and 4. By trial and improvement calculate a solution to 2 decimal places.

x	$x^3 + 2x$	Comment

Answer: ....

3 A rectangular box has the following dimensions:

x cm, x cm, $x + 3$cm

a) Show that the volume of the box is given by the expression $x^3 + 3x^2$.

....

....

b) The volume of the box is 40cm^3. Using trial and improvement, find x which has a value that lies between 2 and 3. Give your answer to 1 decimal place.

x	$x^3 + 3x^2$	Comment

Answer: ....

4 **a)** The equation $x^3 + 10x = 24$ has one solution which lies between 1 and 2. Using trial and improvement, find the solution to 1 decimal place.
   b) The equation $x^3 - 6x = 65$ has one solution which lies between 4 and 5. Using trial and improvement, find the solution to 2 decimal places.

5 A rectangular box has the following dimensions: length = $2x$ cm, width = x cm and height = $x + 3$cm.
   a) Show that the volume of the box is given by the expression $2x^3 + 6x^2$.
   b) The volume of the box is 50cm^3. Using trial and improvement find x, which has a value that lies between 2 and 3. Give your answer to 1 decimal place.

1 a) The first four numbers of a sequence are:

1, 3, 7, 15…

The rule to continue this sequence of numbers is:

**Multiply the previous
number by 2 and
then add 1**

i) What are the next two numbers in the sequence?

....

ii) The following sequence obeys the same rule:

-2, -3, 5, -9…

What are the next two numbers in this sequence?

....

b) The first four numbers of a sequence are:

3, 4, 6, 10…

The rule to continue this sequence of numbers is:

**Subtract 1 from the
previous number and
then multiply by 2**

i) What are the next two numbers in the sequence?

....

ii) The following sequence obeys the same rule:

1, 0, -2, -6…

What are the next two numbers in this sequence?

....

2 a) The first four square numbers are 1, 4, 9 and 16. What are the next four numbers in the sequence?

....

b) The first four triangular numbers are 1, 3, 6 and 10. What are the next four numbers in the sequence?

....

3 The nth term of a sequence is $5n + 8$.

a) What is the value of the 3rd term?

....

b) What is the value of the 10th term?

....

4 The nth term of a sequence is $2n - 11$.

a) What is the value of the 4th term?

....

b) What is the value of the 16th term?

....

5 The nth term of a sequence is $2n - 9$.

a) Which term has a value of 19?

....

....

b) Which term has a value of -5?

....

6 The nth term of a sequence is $7n + 6$.

a) Which term has a value of 69?

....

....

b) Which term has a value of 90?

....

Number Patterns & Sequences 1 & 2

7 The first four terms of a sequence are:

3, 5, 7, 9, ...

Write down a formula for the *n*th term of this sequence and add a further 5 terms to the sequence.

....

....

....

....

8 The first four terms of a sequence are:

6, 4, 2, 0,..

Write down a formula for the *n*th term of this sequence and add a further 5 terms to the sequence.

....

....

....

....

9 Here is a sequence of diagrams made up of squares:

Diagram 1　　**Diagram 2**　　**Diagram 3**　　**Diagram 4**

a) Write down a formula for the number of squares (*s*) in terms of diagram number (*n*).

....

....

....

b) How many squares would there be in Diagram 8?

....

c) Which number diagram would have 49 squares?

....

....

10 Here is a sequence of diagrams made up of circles.

Diagram 1　　**Diagram 2**　　**Diagram 3**　　**Diagram 4**

a) Write down a formula for the number of circles (*c*) in terms of diagram number (*n*).

....

....

....

b) How many circles would there be in Diagram 15?

....

c) Which number diagram would have 81 circles?

....

....

11 Draw the next two diagrams of the following sequences:

a)

b)

```
                              1
                  1        1     1
         1      1   1    1   2   1
   1        1  1  2  1  1  3  3  1
```

12 The *n*th term of a sequence is $\frac{(4n-7)}{3}$ **a)** What is the value of the 10th term? **b)** Which term has a value of 27?

13 The first four terms of a sequence are: 15, 11, 7, 3...

a) Write down a formula for the *n*th term of this sequence. **b)** What is the value of **i)** the 10th term? **ii)** the 100th term?

Plotting Points

1 Write down the coordinates of all the plotted points below.

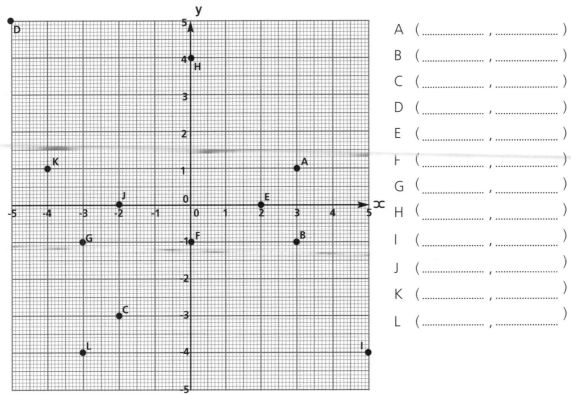

A (..................... , ...)

B (..................... , ...)

C (..................... , ...)

D (..................... , ...)

E (..................... , ...)

F (..................... , ...)

G (..................... , ...)

H (..................... , ...)

I (..................... , ...)

J (..................... , ...)

K (..................... , ...)

L (..................... , ...)

2 Use the axes below to help you answer the following questions:

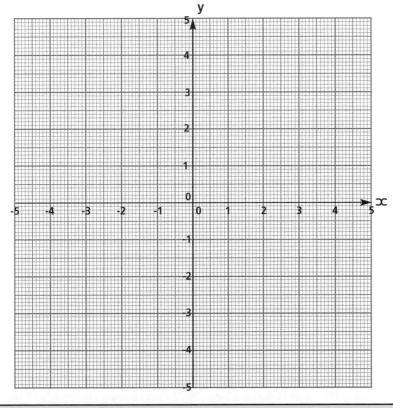

a) The coordinates of 3 points are A (3,0), B (0,-3), C (-3,0). What are the coordinates of point D if ABCD is a square?

....

b) The coordinates of 3 points are P (4,2), Q (3,-2), R (-2,-2). What are the coordinates of point S if PQRS is a parallelogram?

....

c) The coordinates of 3 points are E (1,5), F (4,4), G (1,-3). What are the coordinates of point H if EFGH is a kite?

....

3 The coordinates of 3 points are A (2,3), B (2,-2), C (-3,-2). What are the coordinates of point D if ABCD is a square?

4 The coordinates of 3 points are P (-4,0), Q (3,4), R (4,0). What are the coordinates of point S if PQRS is a kite?

Graphs of Linear Functions 1

1 On the axes provided, draw and label the graphs of the following linear functions for values of x between -2 and 2:

a) $y = 2x$

x	-2	0	2
y	-4	0	4

b) $y = 2x - 1$

x	-2	0	2
y	-5		

c) $y = x + 2$

x			
y			

d) $y = -2x$

x			
y			

e) $y = -x - 3$

x			
y			

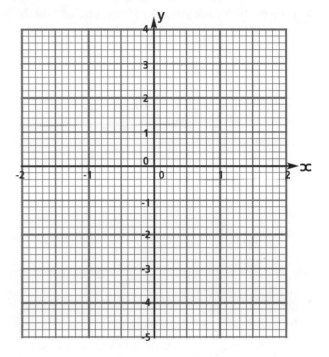

2 **a)** Make y the subject of the following function:

$2y - x = 8$

....

....

b) On the axes provided, draw and label the graph of the rearranged function from part a).

x			
y			

c) A point, which lies on the line of the graph that you have just drawn, has the coordinates (5,p). Calculate the value of p.

....

....

d) Another point that lies on the line of the drawn graph has the coordinates (q,0). Calculate the value of q.

....

....

3 **a)** Make y the subject of the following function: $y - 3x = -4$
b) Draw the graph of the rearranged function for values of x between -3 and 3.
c) Use the graph to calculate the value of y if $x = 1.5$
d) Use the graph to calculate the value of x if y = 3.2

4 **a)** Draw graphs of $y = 3x$ and $y = x + 5$ for values of x between 0 and 4 on the same set of axes.
b) What is the x coordinate of the point where the two lines cross?
c) Now solve the equation $3x = x + 5$.

Graphs of Linear Functions 2

1 Find the gradient and intercept of the following linear functions:

a) $y = 2x + 1$

....

....

....

b) $y = 3x - 1$

....

....

....

c) $x + y = 3$

....

....

....

d) $4y = 7 - 8x$

....

....

....

e) $2y - 2x = 9$

....

....

....

f) $2x = y - 2$

....

....

....

2 Four of the equations from question 1 have been plotted below. What is the equation of each line?

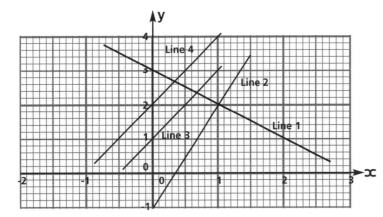

Line 1: ....

Line 2: ....

Line 3: ....

Line 4: ....

3 What is the equation of the line which crosses the y-axis at...

a) $(0,1)$ and is parallel to $y = 2x$? ....

b) $(0,1)$ and is parallel to $y = -2x$? ....

c) $(0,-2)$ and is parallel to $y = 2x$? ....

d) $(0,-2)$ and is parallel to $y = x + 2$? ....

e) $(0,3)$ and is perpendicular to $y = -x - 3$? ....

f) $(0,-3.5)$ and is perpendicular to $y = -x$? ....

---

4 Find the gradient and intercept of the following linear functions:
a) $y = -3x - 3$ **b)** $4y = 3x + 8$ **c)** $2y - x = 3$ **d)** $x - 2y = 3$ **e)** $2y - 3 = x$ **f)** $\dfrac{y - 2x}{3} = 5$ **g)** $\dfrac{y + 4x}{5} = 1$

5 What is the equation of the line which crosses the y-axis at **a)** $(0,4)$ and is parallel to $y = x - 4$, **b)** $(0,0)$ and is perpendicular to $y = x - 4$

6 Which of the following linear functions would produce parallel lines if drawn on the same axes:
i) $y = 2x + 3$ **ii)** $y + 2x = 3$ **iii)** $2y - 4x = 7$ **iv)** $y - 6 = 2x$

7 Which of the following linear functions would produce perpendicular lines if drawn on the same axes:
i) $y - 2x = 4$ **ii)** $3x + y = 7$ **iii)** $3y - x = 4$ **iv)** $3y + 3x = 5$

Graphs of Linear Functions 3

1 Find the gradient, intercept and equation of the following lines:

a)

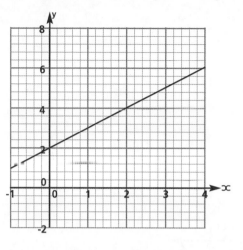

....
....
....
....
....
....

b)

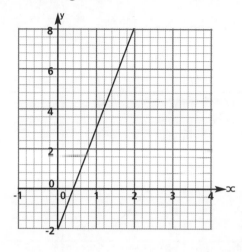

....
....
....
....
....

c)

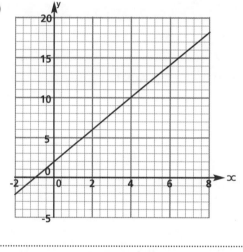

....
....
....
....
....

d)

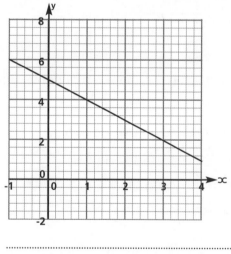

....
....
....
....
....

2 Plot the following points: A(0,1), B(4,5), C(1,4) and D(4,1).
   a) Calculate the gradient of **i)** line AB, **ii)** line CD, **b)** What is the equation of **i)** line AB, **ii)** line CD?

3 A line has intercept c = +2. A point with coordinates (4,4) lies on the line. What is the equation of the line?

4 A line has intercept c = +5. A point with coordinates (4,1) lies on the line. What is the equation of the line?

Three Special Graphs

1 On the axes below are the graphs of 6 lines. What is the equation of each line?

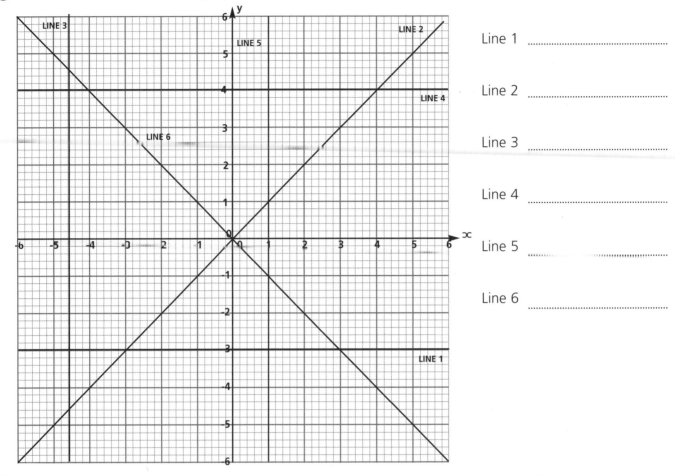

Line 1 ....

Line 2 ....

Line 3 ....

Line 4 ....

Line 5 ....

Line 6 ....

2 **a)** Two points which lie on the line of a drawn graph have coordinates (-3,0) and (4,0).

What is the equation of the line? ....

b) Two points which lie on the line of a drawn graph have coordinates (-1,5) and (-1,3).

What is the equation of the line? ....

c) Two points which lie on the line of a drawn graph have coordinates (-4,4) and (4,-4).

What is the equation of the line? ....

3 **What is the equation of the line that passes through the point with coordinates (3,3) and has a gradient of 1?**..

4 **a)** What are the coordinates of the point of intersection of the two lines $y = x$ and $y = -3$?

....

b) What are the coordinates of the point of intersection of the two lines $y = 6$ and $x = -2$?

....

5 What is the equation of the line that is parallel to the x-axis and passes through the point with coordinates (2.5, 3.6)?

6 What is the equation of the line that is perpendicular to the x-axis and passes through the point with coordinates (-2.8, 1.2)?

Linear Inequalities 1 & 2

1 Solve the following inequalities and complete the number line for each one:

a) $x + 2 > 11$

b) $8 > x - 9$

c) $2x + 5 \leqslant 15$

d) $13 \geqslant 5 + 4x$

e) $7x - 2 \leqslant 2x + 13$

f) $6 + 3x < 21 - 2x$

2 Solve the following inequalities:

a) $12 + 3x < 6$

b) $14 > 5 - 3x$

c) $5(4x + 7) \geqslant 15$

d) $3(2x + 5) \geqslant 24$

e) $6(4 - x) \leqslant 9$

f) $8 \geqslant 3 - 2x$

3 Draw, label and shade the region represented by each inequality on the grids provided.

a) $x \geqslant 1$

b) $y < -2$

c) $y > -x + 2$

d) $y \leqslant 2x - 1$

Linear Inequalities 1 & 2 (cont)

4 **a)** On the grid, draw and shade the region that satisfies these three inequalities:

$x \leqslant 3$, $y \leqslant 4$ and $x + y \geqslant 4$

Label the region A.

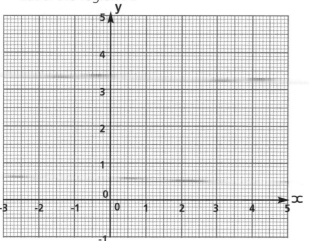

b) B is a point within region A, and has coordinates that are both integers.

What are the coordinates of B?

....

5 **a)** On the grid, draw and shade the region that satisfies these three inequalities:

$x < 4$, $y \geqslant 1$ and $x > y$

Label the region A.

b) B is a point within region A, and has coordinates that are both integers.

What are the coordinates of B?

....

6 On the grid, draw and shade the region that satisfies these four inequalities:

$x > -2$, $y \geqslant 0$, $y \geqslant 0.5x$, $x + y < 3$

Label the region A.

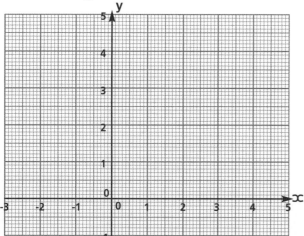

7 On the grid, the region labelled A satisfies four inequalities, what are they?

....

....

....

8 Solve the following inequalities and for each one draw a number line. **a)** $4x \geqslant 20$ **b)** $x + 3 > 5$ **c)** $4x - 3 \leqslant 19$
  d) $8x + 5 < 2x - 7$ **e)** $5(2x - 3) < 4x + 9$ **f)** $7(3x - 2) \geqslant 20x - 16$ **g)** $6(3x - 2) < 4(4x - 10)$

9 On a suitable grid, draw and shade the region that satisfies these three inequalities:
  $x \geqslant 2$, $y \leqslant 5$ and $y \geqslant x$. Label the region A.

10 On a suitable grid, draw and shade the region that satisfies these four inequalities:
  $x > -1$, $y \geqslant x - 2$, $y > -1$ and $y \leqslant -x + 5$. Label the region A.

Simultaneous Equations 1

1 Solve the following simultaneous equations:

a) $2x + y = 8$

$x + y = 5$

b) $2x + 5y = 24$

$3x - 5y = 11$

c) $x - 6y = 17$

$3x + 2y = 11$

d) $4x + 3y = 27$

$x + y = 7$

e) $5x - 2y = 14$

$2x + 3y = 17$

f) $3x + 4y = 13$

$2x - 3y = 3$

2 At break time a student buys two doughnuts and a coffee, which costs her 84p altogether. At lunchtime, the same student buys three doughnuts and two coffees, which cost 138p altogether. Form two equations with the information given and work out the individual price of a doughnut (d) and a coffee (c).

3 Solve the following simultaneous equations:

a) $5x + y = 14$, $3x + y = 10$ **b)** $4x - y = 6$, $x + y = 9$ **c)** $3x + 2y = 8$, $x + y = 2$ **d)** $4x + 6y = 12$, $x + y = 1$

e) $4x + 2y = 13$, $10x - 4y = 1$ **f)** $x - 10y = 2$, $4x + 2y = -13$ **g)** $4x - 3y = -6$, $y - 3x = 7$ **h)** $10x + 2y = 0$, $x - y = 9$

Simultaneous Equations 2

1 a) On the axes below, draw and label the graph of the following equations:

$y = x + 8$ and $y = 2x + 5$

x	0	2	4
y=x+8	8	10	12

x	0	2	4
y=2x+5	5	9	13

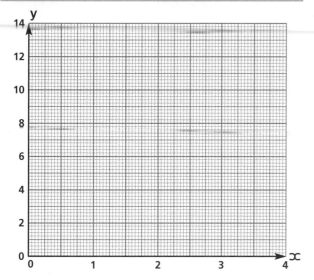

b) Use your graph to solve the simultaneous equations: $y = x + 8$ and $y = 2x + 5$

....

2 a) On the axes below, draw and label the graph of the following equations:

$y = 3x + 10$ and $y = -x + 22$

x	0	2	4
y=3x+10			

x	0	2	4
y=-x+22			

b) Use your graph to solve the simultaneous equations: $y = 3x + 10$ and $y = -x + 22$

....

3 a) On the axes provided draw the graphs of the following lines:

i) $y = -x + 4$

ii) $y = x + 2$

iii) $y = -0.25x + 1$

b) Use your graph to solve the following simultaneous equations:

i) $y = x + 2$ and $y = -0.25x + 1$...........................

ii) $y = x + 2$ and $y = -x + 4$ ....

iii) $y = -x + 4$ and $y = -0.25x + 1$........................

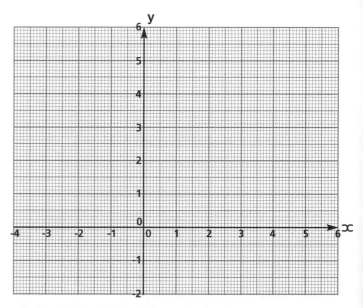

4 a) Draw the graph of $2x + y = 13$ and $3x = y - 3$ for values of x between 0 and 4.
b) Use your graph to solve the simultaneous equations $2x + y = 13$ and $3x = y - 3$.

5 a) Draw the graph of $x + y = 6$, $3x - y = 2$ and $x - y = 4$ for values of x between -2 and 6.
b) Use your graph to solve the following simultaneous equations: **i)** $x + y = 6$, $3x - y = 2$ **ii)** $x + y = 6$, $x - y = 4$.
iii) $3x - y = 2$, $x - y = 4$

Simultaneous Equations 3 & 4

1 **Solve these simultaneous equations (to 1 d.p.)**

a) $y = 3 - 14x$ and $y = 5x^2$

b) $y = 10x^2$ and $y = x + 24$

....

....

....

....

....

....

....

....

....

....

....

....

....

2 **Solve these simultaneous equations by substitution. If need be give your answers to 1 d.p.**

a) $x^2 + y^2 = 1$ and $x + y = 1$

b) $x^2 + y^2 = 9$ and $x + y = 2$

....

....

....

....

....

....

....

....

....

....

....

....

Simultaneous Equations 3 & 4

3 **a)** Using the axes opposite solve graphically the simultaneous equations $y - x = 1$ and $y = x^2$

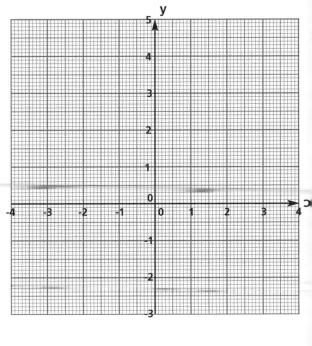

....

....

....

b) Check your answers to part **a)** by solving the simultaneous equations by substitution.

....

....

....

4 **Using the axes opposite solve graphically these pairs of simultaneous equations:**

a) $x^2 + y^2 = 9$

$y - x = 2$

b) $x^2 + y^2 = 9$

$x + y = 2$

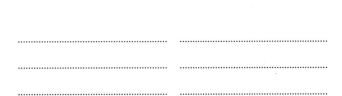

....

....

....

5 **Solve these simultaneous equations.**
a) By substitution **b)** Graphically. If need be give your answer to 1 d.p.
i) $y = 2x^2$ **ii)** $y = \frac{1}{2}x^2$ **iii)** $y = x^2$
$y - x = 2$ $x + y = 1$ $x + y = 1$

6 **Solve graphically the following simultaneous equations:**
a) $x^2 + y^2 = 4$ **b)** $x^2 + y^2 = 9$ **c)** $x^2 + y^2 = 1$
$y = 2x$ $y = -x + 2$ $y = \frac{1}{2}x^2$

Graphs of Quadratic Funcs. 1 & 2

1 Below is a table of values for $y = x^2 - 2$.

x	-2	-1	0	1	2
y	2	-1	-2	-1	2

a) Draw the graph of $y = x^2 - 2$.

b) From your graph find the value(s) of…

i) y when $x = 1.5$

....

ii) x when $y = 1.5$

....

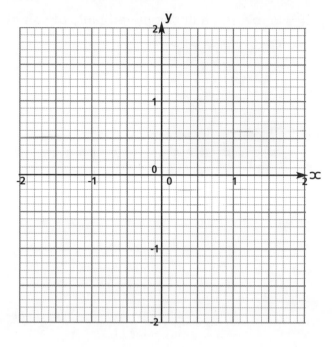

2 Below is a half completed table of values for
$y = x^2 + x - 3$.

a) Complete the table.

x	-3	-2	-1	0	1	2
x^2		4		0		4
$+x$		-2		0		2
-3		-3		-3		-3
$y = x^2 + x - 3$		-1		-3		3

b) Draw the graph of $y = x^2 + x - 3$.

c) From your graph find the value(s) of…

i) y when $x = -2.5$

....

ii) x when $y = 1.6$

....

d) From your graph find the solution to the
equation $x^2 + x - 3 = 0$.

....

e) From your graph find the solution to the
equation $x^2 + x - 3 = 1$.

....

f) From your graph find the solution to the
equation $x^2 + x - 3 = -2$.

....

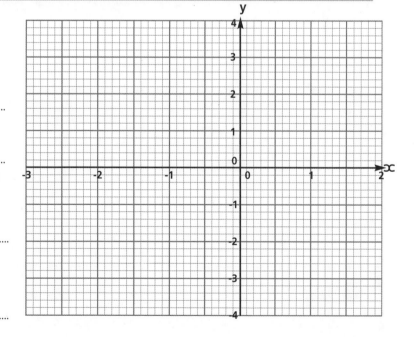

❸ **Below is a half completed table of values for y = $x^2 + 2x - 4$.**

x	-4	-3	-2	-1	0	1	2
x^2		9		1		1	
$+2x$		-6		-2		2	
-4		-4		-4		-4	
y = $x^2 + 2x - 4$		-1		-5		-1	

a) Complete the table.

b) Draw the graph of $y = x^2 + 2x - 4$.

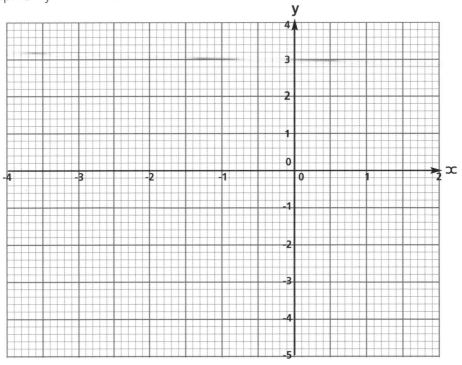

c) From your graph find the solutions to the equations…

i) $x^2 + 2x - 4 = 0$

....

....

....

....

ii) $x^2 + 2x - 6 = 0$

....

....

....

....

iii) $x^2 + 2x = 1$

....

....

....

....

❹ **a)** Draw a table of results for $y = x^2 + 4x - 6$ for values of x between -6 and 2.
b) Draw the graph of $y = x^2 + 4x - 6$.
c) From your graph find the solutions to the equations: **i)** $x^2 + 4x - 6 = 0$ **ii)** $x^2 + 4x - 9 = 0$ **iii)** $x^2 + 4x + 2 = 0$

❺ **a)** Draw the graph of $y = x^2 - 12$ for values of x between -4 and 4.
b) From your graph find the solutions to the equations: **i)** $x^2 - 12 = 0$ **ii)** $x^2 = 15$ **iii)** $x^2 - 6 = 0$

❻ **a)** Draw the graph of $y = x^2 - x - 8$ for values of x between -3 and 4.
b) From your graph find the solutions to the equations: **i)** $x^2 - x - 8 = 0$ **ii)** $x^2 - x - 8 = -2$ **iii)** $x^2 - x - 8 = 3$

Graphs of Other Functions 1

1 Below is a half completed table of values for $y = x^3 + 10$.

a) Complete the table.

x	-3	-2	-1	0	1	2
x^3		-8		0		8
+10		+10		+10		+10
$y = x^3 + 10$		2		10		18

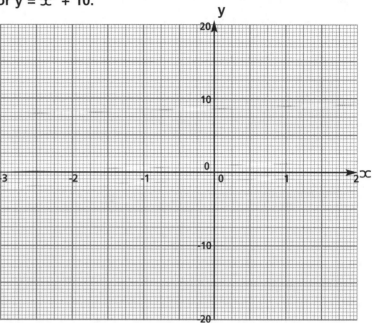

b) On the axes opposite draw the graph of $y = x^3 + 10$.

c) Use your graph to find...

i) the value of x, when $y = -10$

....

ii) the value of y, when $x = 1.5$

....

2 Below is a table of values for $y = \frac{1}{x}$ with $x \neq 0$.

x	-5	-4	-3	-2	-1	-0.5	-0.$\dot{3}$	-0.25	-0.2
$y = \frac{1}{x}$	-0.2	-0.25	-0.$\dot{3}$	-0.5	-1	-2	-3	-4	-5

x	0.2	0.25	0.$\dot{3}$	0.5	1	2	3	4	5
$y = \frac{1}{x}$	5	4	3	2	1	0.5	0.$\dot{3}$	0.25	0.2

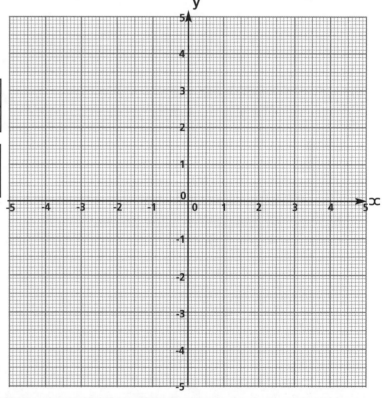

a) On the axes opposite draw the graph of $y = \frac{1}{x}$ with $x \neq 0$.

b) Use your graph to find...

i) the value of x when $y = 2.5$ ....

ii) the value of y when $x = -1.5$ ....

3 Below is a half completed table of values for $y = x^3 - 2$.

x	-3	-2	-1	0	1	2	3
x^3		-8		0		8	
-2		-2		-2		-2	
$y = x^3 - 2$		-10		-2		6	

a) Complete the table.

b) Draw the graph of $y = x^3 - 2$.

c) Use your graph to find the value of x, when $y = 0$

d) Use your graph to find...

i) the value of x when $y = 20$

ii) the value of y when $x = 1.5$

Graphs of Other Functions 2

1 a) For values of x from -2 to 2 complete the tables below.

x	-2	-1	0	1	2
4^x					

x	-2	-1	0	1	2
$\left(\frac{1}{4}\right)^x$					

b) Draw graphs of $y = 4^x$ and $y = \left(\frac{1}{4}\right)^x$ on the same axes opposite.

c) What do you notice about the graphs of the two functions?

....

....

....

....

2 a) The table below shows values of x and y for the relationship $y = ab^x$.

x	0	1	2	3
y	10	20	40	80

b) Using the axes opposite draw the graph of the relationship $y = ab^x$.

c) Use the graph to find the values of **a** and **b** and the relationship.

....

....

....

....

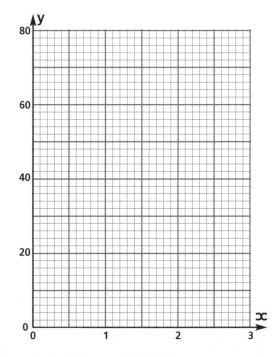

---

3 Draw the graphs of the following exponential functions for values of x from 0 to 4.
 a) $y = 4^x$ **b)** $y = 3 \times 0.5^x$ **c)** $y = -1 \times 2^x$

4 A graph fits the relationship $y = ab^x$. When $x = 0$, y = 2 and when $x = 2$, y = 18.
 a) Find the values of a and b and hence the relationship.
 b) Draw the graph of this relationship.

Graphs of Other Functions 3

1 a) Complete this table of values for the graph of y = sinɔ.

ɔ (°)	0	30	60	90	120	150	180	210	240	270	300	330	360
y = sinɔ													

b) On the grid opposite carefully plot the points and draw the graph of y = sinɔ.

c) Use your graph to estimate two angles which have sinɔ = 0.8

....

d) Use your graph to estimate sin 45°.

....

2 a) Complete this table of values for the graph of y = cosɔ .

ɔ (°)	0	30	60	90	120	150	180	210	240	270	300	330	360
y = cosɔ													

b) On the grid opposite carefully plot the points and draw the graph of y = cosɔ.

c) Use your graph to estimate two angles which have cosɔ = 0.6

....

d) Use your graph to estimate cos 315°.

....

3 a) On a suitable grid draw the graph of y = tan ɔ for values of ɔ from 0° to 360°.

b) In which ways is the graph of y = tan ɔ similar and different to the graphs of y = sinɔ and y = cosɔ.

Transformations of Functions 1

1 a) On the axes opposite draw and label the graph
of $y = x^2$ for values of x from -3 to 3.

b) On the same axes, sketch and label the graphs of...

  i) $y = x^2 - 4$

  ii) $y = 3x^2$

c) i) Describe carefully the transformation that
  maps $y = x^2$ onto $y = x^2 - 4$

....

....

....

  ii) Describe carefully the transformation that
  maps $y = x^2$ onto $y = 3x^2$

....

....

....

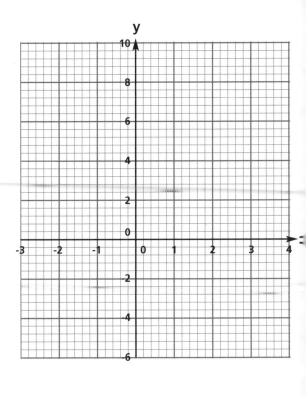

2 a) On the axes opposite draw and label the graph
of $y = x^2$ for values of x from -4 to 4.

b) On the same axes, sketch and label the graphs of...

  i) $y = (x - 3)^2$

  ii) $y = \left(\frac{x}{3}\right)^2$

c) i) Describe carefully the transformation that
  maps $y = x^2$ onto $y = (x - 3)^2$

....

....

....

  ii) Describe carefully the transformation that
  maps $y = x^2$ onto $y = \left(\frac{x}{3}\right)^2$

....

....

....

3 Sketch these graphs on the same axes:

a) $y = x^2$ $y = 4x^2$ $y = x^2 - 1$

b) $y = x^2$ $y = (3x)^2$ $y = (x + 5)^2$

c) $y = x^2$ $y = \frac{1}{3}x^2$ $y = x^2 + 3$

Transformations of Functions 2

1 a) On the same axes below sketch the graphs of **i)** $y = \sin x$ **ii)** $y = \frac{1}{2}\sin x$ and **iii)** $y = \sin 2x$.

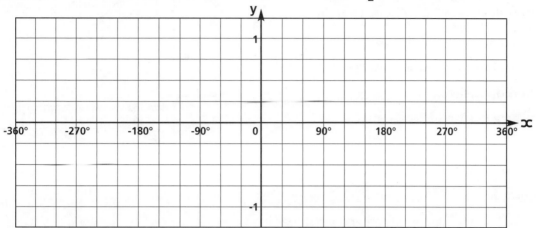

b) Describe the transformation that maps $y = \sin x$ onto…

i) $y = \frac{1}{2}\sin x$ ....

ii) $y = \sin 2x$ ....

2 a) On the same axes below sketch the graphs of **i)** $y = \cos x$ **ii)** $y = \cos(x + 90°)$ and **iii)** $y = \cos x - 3$.

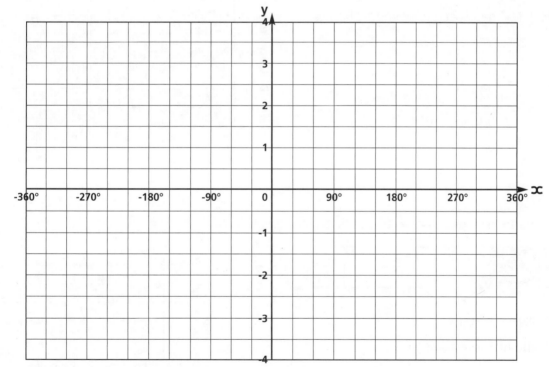

b) Describe the transformation that maps $y = \cos x$ onto…

i) $y = \cos(x + 90°)$ ....

ii) $y = \cos x - 3$ ....

---

3 a) On a suitable set of axes sketch the graphs of $y = \cos x$, $y = 3\cos x$, $y = \cos x + 3$

b) On a suitable set of axes sketch the graphs of $y = \sin x$, $y = \sin\frac{1}{2}x$, $y = \sin(x + 45°)$

Other Graphs 1

❶ Two towns A and B are 100 miles apart.
Mr Brown lives in A and drives to B and
Mr Smith lives in B and drives to A on the
same day, along the same route. Using
the graph opposite…

a) What time did Mr Smith set off?

....

b) Which motorist completed the journey in
the shortest time? ....

c) Who reached the highest speed and what was it? ....

d) What happened at Y? ....

e) Who stopped and for how long? ....

❷ **Here is part of a travel graph of Tina's
journey to the shops and back.**

a) Calculate Tina's speed in km/h for the first
20 mins. ....

....

b) Tina spends 20 mins at the shops, then
travels back home at 48km/h.
Complete her journey on the graph.

❸ **a)** Plot the following data onto this velocity-time graph.

Time (s)	0	1	2	3	4	5	6
Velocity (m/s)	0	5	10	15	20	20	25

b) Calculate the acceleration of the object
over the first 4 seconds.

....

....

❹ An object travels at a constant speed of 20m/s for the first 6 seconds, then accelerates at 5m/s² for another 4
seconds. Draw a graph to show the speed of the object over 10 seconds.

❺ A train leaves town A for town B at 1pm and maintains a steady speed of 60km/h. At 2pm another train leaves
B for A maintaining a speed of 72km/h. The distance between A and B is 180km. Draw the distance-time graphs
for these trains on the same axes. At what time do they pass each other?

Other Graphs 2

1 The cost of hiring a car is £30 plus an extra charge of 30p per mile.

a) Complete this table:

Miles	0	10	20	30	50	100
Cost (£)	30	33				

b) On the axes opposite draw a graph to show the cost of hiring the car for up to 100 miles.

c) Use the graph to estimate how much it would cost to hire a car for an 80 mile journey.

....

2 These sketch graphs show the cost of running a business over several months. Identify which sketch matches each of these descriptions.

a) Costs are rising steadily. ....

b) Costs are falling after reaching a peak. ....

c) Costs are rising at an increasing rate. ....

d) Costs have been rising but are now levelling out. ....

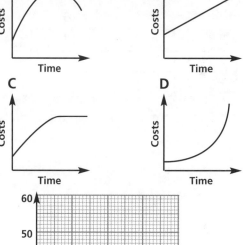

3 **a)** If £1 = $1.4 complete the table to convert pounds sterling (£) to US dollars ($).

Pounds (£)	10	20	30	40
US Dollars ($)				

b) On the axes opposite draw the graph to convert pounds (£) to US dollars ($).

c) Use your graph to convert $30 into pounds.

....

4 Three plumbers A, B and C charge as follows: A – Call out charge £20 then £10 per hour extra.
   B – Call out charge £30 then £5 per hour extra.   C – Standard charge £50 regardless of time.
   a) Draw a graph for each plumber's charges on the same axes, for up to 5 hrs work.
   b) Which plumber is cheapest for a 30 minute job?
   c) Which plumber is cheapest for a $2\frac{1}{2}$ hour job?
   d) After what time will plumber C become the cheapest?

5 A tank of water, cuboid in shape, is being drained out at a rate of 10cm depth per minute. If the water is 60cm deep to start with, draw a graph of time against depth.

Direct & Inverse Proportion

1 The table below gives the number of bacteria, N, in a culture at hourly intervals. The number of bacteria is directly proportional to the time, t (hours).

N	0	10	20	30	40	50
t (hours)	0	1	2	3	4	5

a) Draw the graph of N against t on the axes opposite.

b) What is the relationship between N and t?

....

2 The weight, W (kg), of a metal bar is directly proportional to the square of its diameter, d (cm), when the length of the bar is constant.

a) Complete the table below.

W	0	5	20	45	80	125
d	0	1	2	3	4	5
d²	0					

b) On the axes opposite draw the graph of W against d².

c) Use the graph to find the relationship between W and d.

....

3 The time, t (hours), taken to travel a given distance is inversely proportional to the average speed, s (km/h).

a) Complete the table below.

t	1	2	4	10	20
s	100	50	25	10	5
$\frac{1}{s}$					

b) Plot the graph of t against $\frac{1}{s}$.

c) What is the relationship between t and s?

....

4 The tread, t (mm), of a lorry tyre is inversely proportional to the distance travelled, d (10 000 miles). Values for t and d are given in the table.

t (mm)	10	5	2.5	1
d (10 000 miles)	1	2	4	10

a) Draw a graph of t against $\frac{1}{d}$.

b) Use the relationship between t and d to calculate the tread on a tyre after 80 000 miles.

Angles 1 & 2

1 For each diagram work out the size of angle p and angle q, giving a reason for your answer.

They are not drawn to scale.

a)

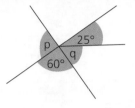

Angle p = ...

Reason: ....

....

Angle q = ...

Reason: ....

....

b)

Angle p = ...

Reason: ....

....

Angle q = ...

Reason: ....

....

c)

Angle p = ...

Reason: ....

....

Angle q = ...

Reason: ....

....

d)

Angle p = ...

Reason: ....

....

Angle q = ...

Reason: ....

....

e)

Angle p = ...

Reason: ....

....

Angle q = ...

Reason: ....

....

f)

Angle p = ...

Reason: ....

....

Angle q = ...

Reason: ....

....

2 For each diagram work out the size of angle c and angle d giving a reason for your answer.

They are not drawn to scale.

a)

Angle c = ...

Reason: ....

....

Angle d = ...

Reason: ....

....

b)

Angle c = ...

Reason: ....

....

Angle d = ...

Reason: ....

....

c)

Angle c = ...

Reason: ....

....

Angle d = ...

Reason: ....

....

Angles 1 & 2 (cont)

3 For each diagram work out the size of angle m and angle n giving a reason for your answer. They are not drawn to scale.

a)

b)

c)

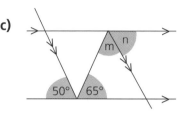

Angle m = ...

Reason: ....

....

Angle n = ...

Reason: ....

....

Angle m = ...

Reason: ....

....

Angle n = ...

Reason: ....

....

Angle m = ...

Reason: ....

....

Angle n = ...

Reason: ....

....

4 Work out the size of the angles marked a, b and c, giving reasons for your answer. The diagram is not drawn to scale.

....

....

....

....

5 Work out the size of the angles marked p, q, r and s, giving reasons for your answer. The diagram is not drawn to scale.

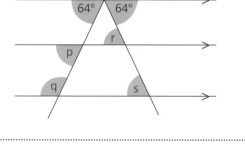

....

....

....

....

6 For each diagram work out the size of x. They are not drawn to scale.

a)

b)

c)

d)

7 For each diagram work out the size of the angles marked giving reasons for your answer. They are not drawn to scale.

a)

b)

c)

Angles in Triangles

1 Draw a diagram and write a short explanation to prove that the interior angles of a triangle add up to 180°.

....

....

....

....

....

2 Draw a diagram and write a short explanation to prove that the exterior angle of a triangle is equal to the sum of the interior angles at the other two vertices.

....

....

....

....

....

3 This diagram has six angles marked a, b, c, d, e and f.

a) Work out the size of angle a in terms of angle b.

b) Work out the size of angle a in terms of angles d and f.

c) What do angles a, c and e add up to?

d) Work out the size of angle a in terms of angles c and e.

Types of Triangle

① Below are four triangles. For each triangle work out the missing angle x and name the type of triangle, giving a reason for your answer. They are not drawn to scale.

a)

b)

c)

d)

Angle x =........................

Angle x =........................

Angle x =........................

Angle x =........................

Type of Triangle:

Type of Triangle:

Type of Triangle:

Type of Triangle:

....

....

....

....

Reason:

Reason:

Reason:

Reason:

....

....

....

....

....

....

....

....

② For each diagram below work out the size of angle p. They are not drawn to scale.

a)

b)

c)

d)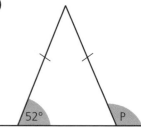

Angle p =........................

Angle p =........................

Angle p =........................

Angle p =........................

③ The diagram (not drawn to scale) shows a right-angled triangle ABC and an isosceles triangle CDE. Work out the size of the angles marked a and b giving reasons for your answers.

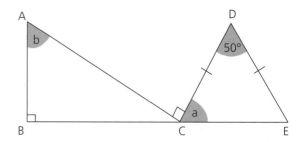

....

....

④ The diagram (not drawn to scale) shows an equilateral triangle ABC and a right-angled triangle CDE. Work out the size of the angles marked m and n giving reasons for your answers.

Quadrilaterals

1 Below are four quadrilaterals. For each quadrilateral work out the missing angle x and name the type of quadrilateral, giving a reason for your answer. They are not drawn to scale.

a)

Angle x = ...

Type of Quadrilateral:

....

Reason:

....

....

b)

Angle x = ...

Type of Quadrilateral:

....

Reason:

....

....

c)

Angle x = ...

Type of Quadrilateral:

....

Reason:

....

....

d)

Angle x = ...

Type of Quadrilateral:

....

Reason:

....

....

2 Which type of quadrilateral am I?

a) I have diagonals that are not equal in length but they bisect each other at right-angles.

....

b) I have diagonals that are equal in length and bisect each other. However they do not bisect each other at right-angles.

....

c) I have diagonals that are equal in length and bisect each other at right-angles.

....

3 Draw a diagram and write a short explanation to prove that the interior angles of a quadrilateral add up to 360°.

....

....

....

....

....

4 Calculate the size of the labelled angles in the following diagrams. They are not drawn to scale.

a)

b)

c)

d)

5 **a)** The interior angles of a quadrilateral are $x°$, $2x°$, $3x°$ and $4x°$. Work out the difference in size between the largest angle and the smallest angle in the quadrilateral.

b) The interior angles of a quadrilateral are $x+20°$, $x-30°$, $2x°$ and 110°. Work out the size of x.

Irregular & Regular Polygons

1 For each diagram below work out the size of angle p. They are not drawn to scale.

a)

b)

....

....

....

2 **a)** What do the exterior angles of an irregular pentagon add up to?.....................................

    b) What do the exterior angles of a regular pentagon add up to?.....................................

3 **An irregular polygon has exterior angles equal to 110°, 94°, 88° and 68°.**

    a) How many sides does the polygon have? ....

    b) What is the sum of the interior angles of this irregular polygon?

....

....

4 **An irregular polygon has interior angles equal to 110°, 155°, 135°, 95°, 140° and 85°.**

    a) How many sides does the polygon have? ....

    b) What is the sum of the exterior angles of this irregular polygon?

....

....

5 **An irregular pentagon has four exterior angles equal to 47°, 113°, 55° and 71°. What is the size of the fifth exterior angle?**

....

6 **a)** How many sides does a polygon have if the sum of its interior angles is twice the sum of its exterior angles? ....

    b) How many sides does a regular polygon have if each interior angle is equal to each exterior angle?

....

    c) How many sides does a polygon have if the sum of its interior angles is equal to the sum of its exterior angles? ....

Irregular & Regular Polygons

7 **A regular polygon has five sides.**

Calculate the size of **a)** each exterior angle and **b)** each interior angle.

....

....

....

....

....

8 **A regular polygon has six sides.**

Calculate the size of **a)** each exterior angle and **b)** each interior angle.

....

....

....

....

....

9 **The diagrams below show regular polygons, centre 0. For each polygon work out the size of the angles marked a and b.**

a)

b)

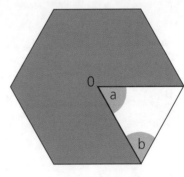

....

....

....

....

10 **Jon reckons that it is possible to have a regular polygon where each interior angle is equal to 150° and each exterior angle is equal to 40°. Is he correct? Explain.**

....

....

11 **A polygon has interior angles equal to $x°$, $x + 20°$, $2x°$, $2x - 10°$ and 50°.**
   a) How many sides does this polygon have?
   b) Work out the size of x.
   c) What is the size of each exterior angle?

12 **A regular polygon has each interior angle equal to $1\frac{1}{2}$ times each exterior angle.**
   a) What is the size of each interior angle?
   b) What is the size of each exterior angle?
   c) How many sides does this regular polygon have?

13 **A regular polygon has each interior angle equal to 170°. How many sides does it have?**

Congruence & Tessellation

1 Which three triangles are congruent? They are not drawn to scale.

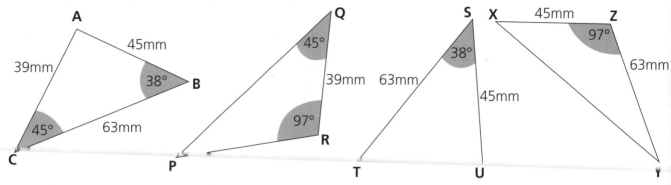

....

....

2 Which of the following pairs of triangles, A and B, are congruent? For each pair that is congruent, give the reason why e.g. SAS, SSS, ASA, RHS. They are not drawn to scale.

a)

....

....

b)

....

....

c)

....

....

d)

....

....

e)

....

....

f)

....

....

g)

....

....

3 PQRS is a square. A and B are points on QR and SR such that QA = SB. Use congruent triangles to prove that $P\hat{A}Q = P\hat{B}S$.

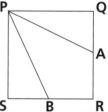

....

....

4 Here are three triangles (not drawn to scale). Which two triangles are congruent? Explain.

5 A regular hexagon will form a tessellation pattern but a regular pentagon does not. Explain why.

6 Using congruent triangles, prove that the line drawn from the centre of a circle through the midpoint of a chord is the perpendicular bisector of the chord.

Similarity

1 Here are four triangles (not drawn to scale).

A   B   C   D

a) Pam thinks that triangles B and C are similar. Is she correct? Explain.

....

....

b) Ian thinks that triangles A and D are similar. Is he correct? Explain.

....

....

2 These two triangles are similar. Calculate the length of...

a) XY ....

b) BC ....

3 In the diagram below BC is parallel to DE. AB = 3 cm, AC = 4cm, BC = 5cm and CE = 2cm.

The diagram is not drawn to scale.

a) Calculate the length of DE.

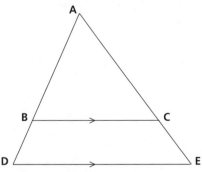

....

....

....

b) Calculate the length of BD.

....

....

....

4 Here are three triangles (not drawn to scale).
Which two triangles are similar? Explain.

Pythagoras' Theorem 1 & 2

1 Use Pythagoras' Theorem to calculate the unknown side in each of the following triangles. They are not drawn to scale. If need be, give your answer to 1 decimal place.

a)

b)

c)

d)

e)

f)

2 Which of the following triangles is not a right-angled triangle? Show all your workings. They are not drawn to scale.

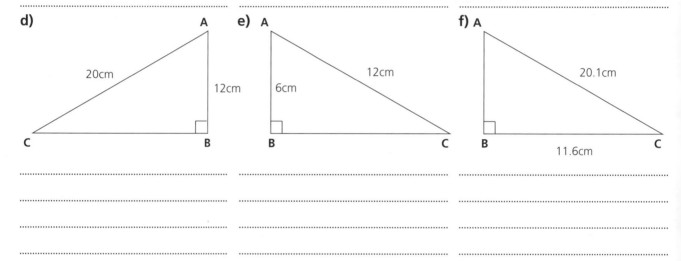

Triangle A

Triangle B

Triangle C

3 Calculate the height of the isosceles triangle alongside, the sides of which measure 10cm, 10cm and 5cm. Give your answer to 2 significant figures. The triangle is not drawn to scale.

4 Look at the diagram below (not drawn to scale). Use Pythagoras' Theorem to calculate...

a) the length of AC.

....

....

....

b) the length of AE to 1 decimal place.

....

....

....

....

....

5 The diagram below shows the position of three villages. It is not drawn to scale. Use Pythagoras' Theorem to calculate the direct distance from Lampton to Campton to 1 decimal place.

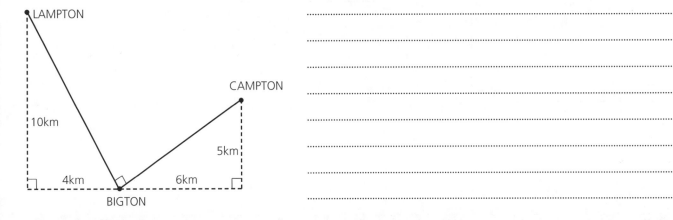

....

....

....

....

....

....

....

....

6 The diagram opposite shows a right-angled triangle ABC.
Use Pythagoras' theorem to calculate...
a) the length of AB to 1 decimal place if BC = 80cm and AC = 1.3m.
b) the length of AC to 1 decimal place if AB = 10cm and the area of triangle ABC is 25cm^2.
c) the length of AB to 1 decimal place if AB = BC and AC = 14.2cm.

7 Triangle ABC has AB = 1.75cm, BC = 6cm and AC = 6.25cm. Is triangle ABC a right-angled triangle? Explain your answer.

8 A square has an area of 36cm^2. Calculate the length of its diagonal to 1 decimal place.

9 A rectangle has an area of 36cm^2 and the length of its base is twice that of its height. Calculate the length of its diagonal.

10 A 4.5m ladder leans against a wall. The foot of the ladder is 1.5m from the base of the wall.
a) How high up the wall does the ladder reach? Give your answer to 1 decimal place.
b) The position of the ladder is now changed so that the distance from the foot of the ladder to the base of the wall is the same as the distance the ladder reaches up the wall. How high up the wall does the ladder now reach, to 1 decimal place?

11 The length of the diagonal of a rectangle is 12cm. The length of its base is three times that of its height. Calculate the length of the base.

Trigonometry 1, 2 & 3

1 Use trigonometry to calculate the length of...

a) BC

$\theta = 30 \quad H = 10$

$\operatorname{Sin} 30 = \dfrac{BC}{10} \times 10$

$= 10 \operatorname{Sin} 30 = BC$
$= 5$

b) AB to 3 significant figures.

$\cos 20° = \dfrac{x}{12} \times 12$

$12 \cos 20° = x$

$x = 11.3$

c) AB to 1 decimal place.

2 Use trigonometry to calculate the size of angle θ in the following triangles. If need be, give your answer to 1 decimal place.

a)

b)

c)

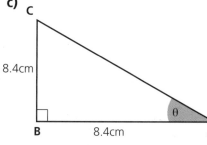

3 Which of the following triangles is right-angled? Show all your workings.

They are not drawn to scale.

4 The tree in the diagram is 4.2m high. From A the angle of elevation to the top of the tree is 30.4°

a) Calculate the distance from A to the base of the tree, B, to 1 decimal place.

....

....

....

b) The angle of elevation of the tree is now measured from a position 2m closer to the tree. Calculate the angle of elevation, to 1 decimal place.

....

....

....

5 The angle of depression from the top of one vertical pole to the top of another vertical pole is 24.5° The height of one pole is 20m and the other is 15m. How far apart are the poles to 1 decimal place?

....

....

....

....

....

....

....

....

....

6 Triangle ABC is a right-angled triangle with $B\hat{A}C = 90°$.
Use trigonometry to calculate...
a) Angle ABC to 1 decimal place if AB = 70cm and BC = 1.6m.
b) Angle ABC to 1 decimal place if the length of AC is twice the length of AB.
c) The length of AB to 1 decimal place if AC = 14cm and angle ACB is four times the size of angle ABC.

7 Triangle ABC has AB = 12.6cm, BC = 6.3cm and angle ACB = 60°.
Is triangle ABC a right-angled triangle? Explain your answer.

8 **a)** The angle of elevation of the top of a tower from a point 30m away from the foot of the tower is 48.2° Calculate the height of the tower to 1 decimal place.
b) The tower has a flag and the angle of elevation of the top of the flag from the same point is 50.4° Calculate the height of the flag to 1 decimal place.

9 The diagram (not drawn to scale) shows a picture hanging on a wall. AD = 3m, AB = 1.4m and CD = 1.8m.
Calculate the height and width of the picture.

B

C

A   40°   20°   D

Problems Involving 3-D Figures

1 **The diagram opposite shows a cube of side 6cm.**

a) Calculate the length of AC. Give your answer to 2 significant figures.

....
....
....

b) Calculate the length of AG. Give your answer to 2 significant figures.

....
....
....
....
....
....

c) Calculate the size of the angle line AG makes with the horizontal base ABCD. Give your answer to 1 decimal place.

....
....
....
....

2 **The diagram opposite shows a triangular prism.**

a) Calculate the length of BC. Give your answer to 2 significant figures.

....
....
....

b) Calculate the length of AE. Give your answer to 2 significant figures.

....
....
....
....
....

c) Calculate the length of CE. Give your answer to 2 significant figures.

....
....
....
....

d) Calculate the angle line BC makes with the horizontal baseline AB. Give your answer to 1 decimal place.

....
....
....
....

e) Calculate the angle line EC makes with the horizontal base ABED. Give your answer to 1 decimal place.

....
....
....
....

Problems Involving 3-D Figures

3 The diagram opposite shows a tent.

AE = BF = DH = CG = 2.4m, AD = EH = 1.8m,

AB = EF = 1.5m and BC = FG = 1.2m.

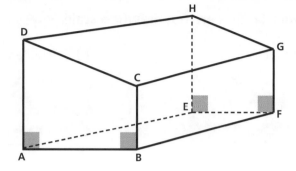

a) Calculate the length of BE.

Give your answer to 3 significant figures.

....

....

....

b) Calculate the length of BH.

Give your answer to 3 significant figures.

....

....

c) Calculate the length of CH.

Give your answer to 3 significant figures.

....

....

d) Calculate the angle line CH makes with

DH. Give your answer to 1 decimal place.

....

....

e) Calculate the angle line CD makes with the

horizontal. Give your answer to 1 decimal place.

....

....

f) Calculate the angle line BH makes with

BE. Give your answer to 1 decimal place.

....

....

g) Calculate the total external surface area, including

the base, of the tent.

....

....

---

4 The diagram shows a square-base pyramid ABCDE, where
AB = BC = CD = DA = 6cm and AE = BE = CE = DE = 10cm.
Point E lies directly above X.

a) Calculate the length of AC.
Give your answer to 2 significant figures.

b) Calculate the length of EX.
Give your answer to 2 significant figures.

c) Calculate the angle line AE makes with the horizontal
base ABCD. Give your answer to 1 decimal place.

5 The diagram shows a cuboid. AB = DC = EF = HG = 3x,
BC = AD = FG = EH = 4x and AE = BF = CG = DH = $\sqrt{7}x$.

a) Calculate the length of AC in terms of x.

b) Calculate the length of AF in terms of x.

c) Calculate the length of AG in terms of x. Leave your
answer in surd form.

d) Calculate the angle line AG makes with the horizontal
base ABCD. Give your answer to 1 decimal place.

e) Calculate the angle line AF makes with the horizontal
base ABCD. Give your answer to 1 decimal place.

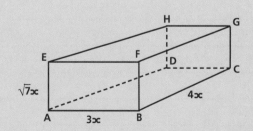

The Sine Rule & Cosine Rule

For questions 1 and 2 use the sine rule only and give your answers to 1 decimal place. The triangles are not drawn to scale.

1 a) Calculate BC

b) Calculate AB

c) Calculate AC

2 a) Calculate AĈB

b) Calculate AB̂C

c) Calculate BÂC

For questions 3 and 4 use the cosine rule only and give your answers to 1 decimal place. The triangles are not drawn to scale.

3 a) Calculate BC

b) Calculate AC

c) Calculate AB

The Sine Rule & Cosine Rule

4 **a)** Calculate BÂC

b) Calculate AB̂C

c) Calculate AĈB

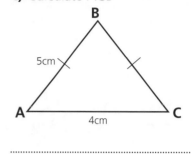

....

....

....

....

....

....

....

....

....

....

....

....

....

....

....

5 A ship sails from Point A due north for 30km to reach Point B. The ship then changes course and sails on a bearing of 110° to reach Point C, which is 45km from Point A, as shown in the diagram.

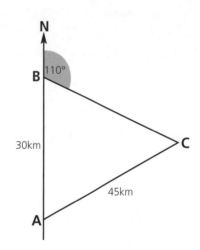

a) Calculate BĈA. Give your answer to 1 decimal place.

....

....

....

b) Calculate the bearing of A from C.

....

c) Calculate the bearing of C from A.

....

d) Calculate the distance BC to 1 decimal place.

....

....

....

6 The direct distance from a post office, P, to a shop, S, is 100m and to a newsagent, N, is 67m. If SN̂P = 85°, calculate... **a)** PŜN and **b)** the distance from the shop to the newsagent. Give your answers to 1 decimal place.

7 Three girls, Alex, Bella and Carrie, stand at three points. The bearing of Bella from Alex is 075° and the bearing of Carrie from Alex is 143°. The distance from Alex to Bella is 165m and the distance from Alex to Carrie is 192m. Calculate **a)** the distance from Bella to Carrie **b)** the bearing of Carrie from Bella and **c)** the bearing of Bella from Carrie. Give your answers to 1 decimal place.

8 The diagram shows the end wall of a house. If the distance from B to D is 6.9m, calculate **a)** BĈD **b)** CB̂D **c)** the distance AE and **d)** the area of the end wall section of the house. Give your answers to 1 decimal place.

Transformations 1

① **The grid shows twelve shapes A to L.**

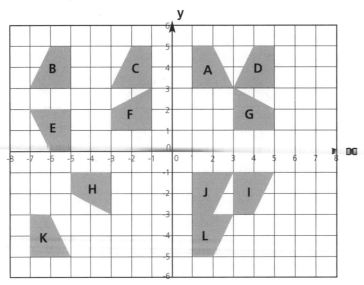

a) Which image is object A reflected…

i) in the x-axis ....

ii) in the y-axis ....

iii) in the line $x = 3$ ....

iv) in the line y = 1 ....

v) in the line y = x ....

vi) in the line y = -x ....

b) Describe the single reflection which takes B to E. ....

c) Describe the single reflection which takes F to G. ....

② **Triangles A, B, C and D are all different reflections of the black triangle. For each one draw in the mirror line and describe the reflection fully.**

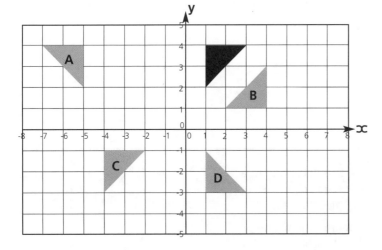

Triangle A: ....

....

Triangle B: ....

....

Triangle C: ....

....

Triangle D: ....

....

③ **A is a triangle with coordinates (3,1), (5,1) and (5,2).**

a) On a suitable grid draw triangle A.

b) i) Reflect triangle A in the line $x = 1$. Label this triangle B. **ii)** Reflect triangle A in the line y = -1. Label this triangle C.

iii) Reflect triangle A in the line y = x. Label this triangle D. **iv)** Reflect triangle A in the line y = -x. Label this triangle E.

Transformations 2

1 **The grid shows ten shapes A to J.**

a) Which image is object A rotated...

i) 90° clockwise about the origin (0,0)

....

ii) 180° clockwise about the origin (0,0)

....

iii) 270° clockwise about the origin (0,0)

....

iv) 90° clockwise about the centre (-2,0)

....

v) 180° clockwise about the centre (-1,1)

....

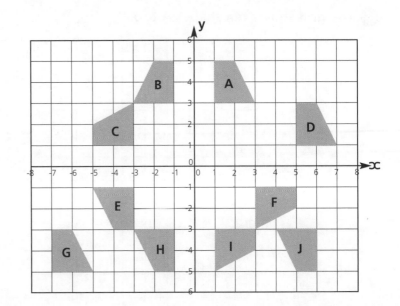

b) Describe the single rotation which takes C to A. ....

c) Describe the single rotation which takes I to A. ....

2 **The grid shows triangle A.**

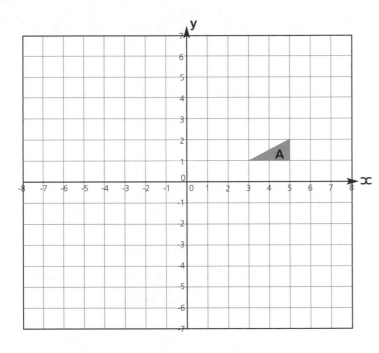

a) Rotate triangle A 90° clockwise about the origin (0,0). Label this triangle B.

b) Rotate triangle A 180° clockwise about the origin (0,0). Label this triangle C.

c) Rotate triangle A 270° clockwise about the origin (0,0). Label this triangle D.

d) Rotate triangle A 90° clockwise about the centre (3,1). Label this triangle E.

e) Rotate triangle A 270° clockwise about the centre (-1,1). Label this triangle F.

3 **A is a quadrilateral with coordinates (2,2), (4,4), (5,3) and (5,1).**

a) On a suitable grid draw quadrilateral A.

b) i) Rotate quadrilateral A 90° clockwise about the origin (0,0). Label this quadrilateral B. ii) Rotate quadrilateral A 180° clockwise about the origin (0,0). Label this quadrilateral C. iii) Rotate quadrilateral A 270° clockwise about the origin (0,0). Label this quadrilateral D. iv) Rotate quadrilateral A 90° clockwise about the centre (2,2). Label this quadrilateral E.

v) Rotate quadrilateral A 180° clockwise about the centre (-1,-1). Label this quadrilateral F.

Transformations 3

1 The grid shows ten shapes A to J.

a) Give the letter of the triangle which is shape A translated by the vector…

i) $\begin{pmatrix} 4 \\ 2 \end{pmatrix}$ ....

ii) $\begin{pmatrix} 1 \\ -4 \end{pmatrix}$ ....

iii) $\begin{pmatrix} -4 \\ 1 \end{pmatrix}$ ....

iv) $\begin{pmatrix} 0 \\ 3 \end{pmatrix}$ ....

v) $\begin{pmatrix} -8 \\ -5 \end{pmatrix}$ ....

vi) $\begin{pmatrix} 4 \\ -6 \end{pmatrix}$ ....

b) What is the translation vector which maps triangle D onto triangle A?...

c) What is the translation vector which maps triangle B onto triangle A? ....

2 The grid shows triangle A. Draw and label the following translations.

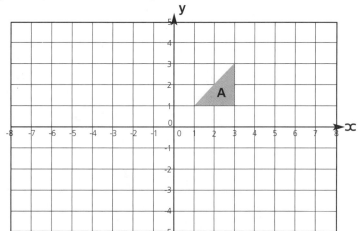

a) Triangle A mapped onto triangle B by the translation vector $\begin{pmatrix} 4 \\ 2 \end{pmatrix}$

b) Triangle A mapped onto triangle C by the translation vector $\begin{pmatrix} -5 \\ -4 \end{pmatrix}$

c) Triangle A mapped onto triangle D by the translation vector $\begin{pmatrix} -8 \\ 0 \end{pmatrix}$

d) Triangle A mapped onto triangle E by the translation vector $\begin{pmatrix} 5 \\ -6 \end{pmatrix}$

3 A is a triangle with coordinates (-1,-3), (-3,-2) and (-4,4).
   a) On a suitable grid draw triangle A.
   b) i) Translate triangle A by the vector $\begin{pmatrix} 5 \\ 5 \end{pmatrix}$ Label this triangle B. **ii)** Translate triangle A by the vector $\begin{pmatrix} -5 \\ -5 \end{pmatrix}$ Label this triangle C.

   iii) Translate triangle A by the vector $\begin{pmatrix} 5 \\ -5 \end{pmatrix}$ Label this triangle D. **iv)** Translate triangle A by the vector $\begin{pmatrix} -5 \\ 5 \end{pmatrix}$ Label this triangle E.

Transformations 4

1 The grid shows triangle A.

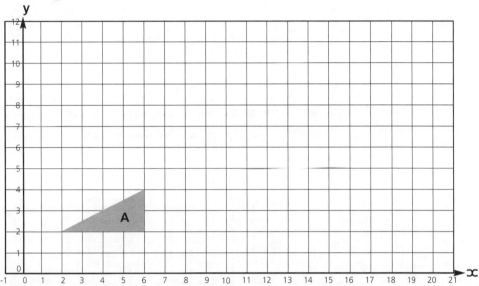

Enlarge triangle A by...

a) a scale factor of 3 about the centre of enlargement (0,0). Label this triangle B.

b) a scale factor of 2 about the centre of enlargement (0,3). Label this triangle C.

c) a scale factor of $\frac{1}{2}$ about the centre of enlargement (0,0). Label this triangle D.

d) a scale factor of 2 about the centre of enlargement (4,0). Label this triangle E.

2 The grid shows three quadrilaterals A, B and C.

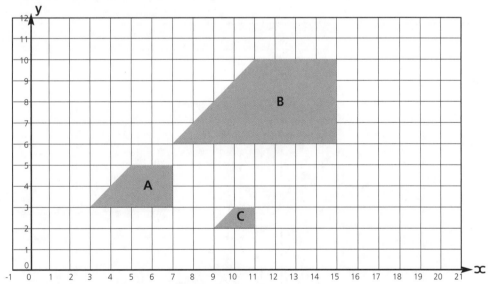

Describe fully the enlargement that would map quadrilateral A...

a) onto B..

b) onto C..

3 Triangle A has coordinates (3,2), (6,2) and (6,4). **a)** On a suitable grid draw triangle A.
b) Complete the following enlargements: **i)** Triangle A is enlarged by a scale factor of 2, centre of enlargement (0,0).
Label this triangle B. **ii)** Triangle A is enlarged by a scale factor of $\frac{1}{2}$, centre of enlargement (0,0). Label this triangle C.
iii) Triangle A is enlarged by a scale factor of 3, centre of enlargement (1,1). Label this triangle D.

Transformations 5

1 On the axes below, draw the enlargement of triangle ABC by...

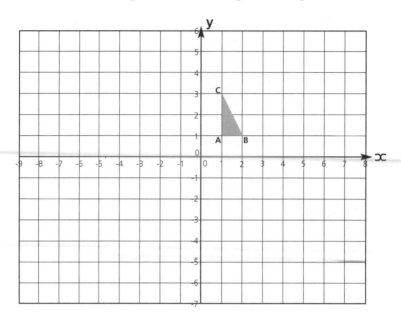

a) scale factor -2, centre (0,0). Label this triangle A'B'C'.

b) scale factor -3, centre (0,1). Label this triangle A"B"C".

c) scale factor -$\frac{1}{2}$, centre (1,0). Label this triangle A'''B'''C'''.

2 Describe fully the transformation that maps triangle P onto...

a) Q ....

b) R ....

c) S ....

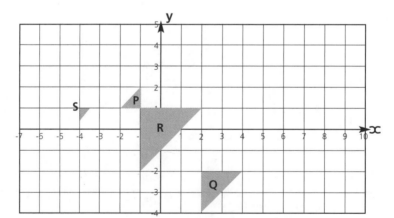

3 **Triangle A has coordinates (-1,1), (-3,1) and (-3,3).**
   a) Using an x-axis and y-axis from -10 to 10, draw triangle A.
   b) Enlarge triangle A by i) scale factor -3, centre (0,0). This is triangle B. ii) scale factor -$\frac{1}{2}$, centre (0,1). This is triangle C.
   c) i) Describe fully the transformation that maps triangle B onto triangle A.
      ii) Describe fully the transformation that maps triangle C onto triangle A.

Transformations 6

1 **The grid shows three triangles A, B and C.**

a) Describe fully a single transformation that would map triangle A onto…

i) triangle B. ....

ii) triangle C. ....

b) Describe fully a single transformation that would map triangle B onto triangle C.

....

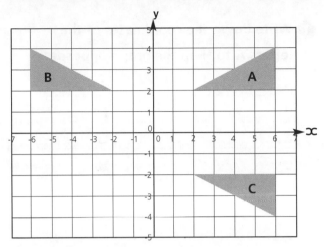

2 **The grid shows three quadrilaterals A, B and C.**

a) Describe fully a single transformation that would map quadrilateral A onto…

i) quadrilateral B ....

ii) quadrilateral C..

b) Describe fully a single transformation that would map quadrilateral B onto quadrilateral C.

....

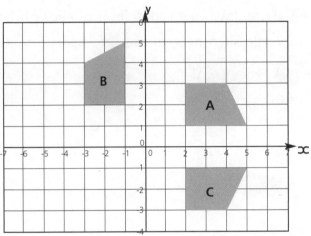

3 **The grid shows triangle A.**

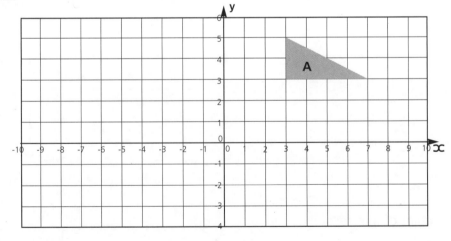

a) Triangle A is reflected in the line $x = 1$. Draw and label this triangle B.

b) Triangle A is reflected in the line y = 1. Draw and label this triangle C.

c) Describe fully the single transformation that would map triangle B onto triangle C.

....

....

4 a) Quadrilateral A has coordinates (3,3), (6,3), (7,6) and (5,6). On a suitable grid draw quadrilateral A.

b) Quadrilateral A is reflected in the line $x = 2$. Draw and label quadrilateral B.

c) Quadrilateral A is reflected in the line y = 0. Draw and label quadrilateral C.

d) Quadrilateral A is rotated 270° clockwise about the origin (0,0). Draw and label quadrilateral D.

e) Describe fully the single transformation that would map quadrilateral B onto quadrilateral C.

f) Describe fully the single transformation that would map quadrilateral D onto quadrilateral C.

Coordinates 1

1 Write down the coordinates of the

letters A to H on the graph opposite.

A .... E ....

B .... F ....

C .... G ....

D .... H ....

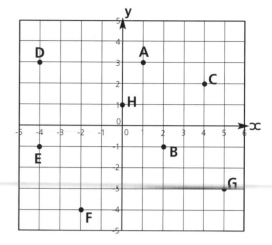

2 Write down the coordinates of each of the

vertices (corners) of this box, apart from (0,0,0).

A .... E ....

B .... F ....

C .... G ....

D ....

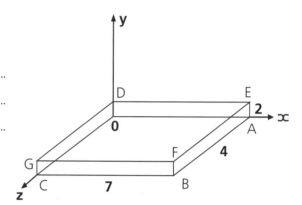

3 This cube has a side length of 5cm.

a) Write down the coordinates of each of the vertices, apart from (0,0,0).

A .... E ....

B .... F ....

C .... G ....

D ....

b) What are the coordinates of the point of intersection

of the two diagonals OB and AC?

....

c) What are the coordinates of the point of intersection

of the two diagonals OF and AG?

....

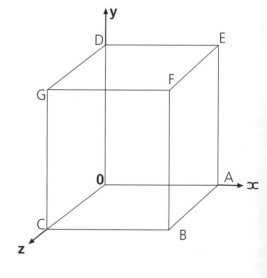

4 Draw axes from -5 to 5 on the x-axis and -3 to 4 on the y-axis.
   a) Draw and label A (4,2), B (-5,2), C (-4,-2) **b)** Draw and label a fourth coordinate D to produce a parallelogram ABCD.

5 The four base coordinates of a cube are (0,0,0), (3,0,0), (3,3,0) and (0,3,0).
   Draw a 3-D graph and write down the other four coordinates.

Coordinates 2

1 **a)** On the graph opposite, plot the coordinates
  A(1,2), B(3,5), C(7,6) and D(7,3).

  b) Find the coordinates of the midpoint, M,
  of the line segments…

  i) AB ....

  ....

  ii) BC ....

  ....

  iii) CD...

  ....

  iv) AD...

  ....

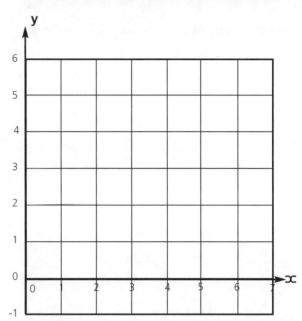

2 **a)** On the graph opposite, plot the coordinates
  P(3,1), Q(0,3), R(4,6), S(7,4).

  b) Calculate the lengths of the line segments…

  i) PQ ....

  ....

  ....

  ....

  ....

  ii) QR ....

  ....

  ....

  ....

  ....

  iii) RS ....   **iv)** SP ....

  ....

  ....

  ....

  ....

3 The line segment AB has coordinates (-2,-1) and (6,4) respectively. Find the coordinates of the midpoint M.

4 Hexagon ABCDEF has coordinates A(-2,3), B(2,3), C(4,0), D(2,-4), E (-2,-4), F(-4,0).
  a) Plot these on a graph to produce a hexagon.
  b) Find the coordinates of the midpoint, M, for line segments: **i)** AF **ii)** BC **iii)** CD **iv)** EF.
  c) Calculate the lengths of the line segments and hence find the perimeter of the hexagon (to 1 d.p.).

Vectors 1 & 2

1 **The diagram below shows eight different vectors.**

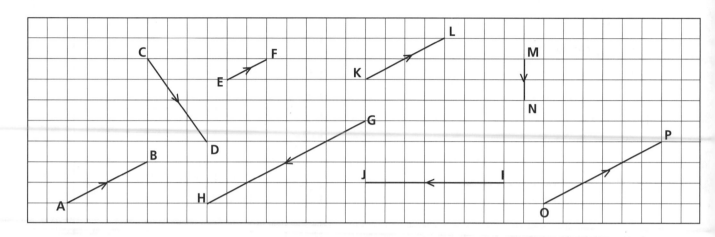

a) Write all the vectors in the diagram in the form $\begin{pmatrix} x \\ y \end{pmatrix}$.

$$\overrightarrow{AB} = \begin{pmatrix} \ \end{pmatrix}, \overrightarrow{CD} = \begin{pmatrix} \ \end{pmatrix}, \overrightarrow{EF} = \begin{pmatrix} \ \end{pmatrix}, \overrightarrow{GH} = \begin{pmatrix} \ \end{pmatrix}, \overrightarrow{IJ} = \begin{pmatrix} \ \end{pmatrix}, \overrightarrow{KL} = \begin{pmatrix} \ \end{pmatrix}, \overrightarrow{MN} = \begin{pmatrix} \ \end{pmatrix}, \overrightarrow{OP} = \begin{pmatrix} \ \end{pmatrix}$$

b) What is the relationship between…

    i) $\overrightarrow{AB}$ and $\overrightarrow{KL}$? ....

    ii) $\overrightarrow{AB}$ and $\overrightarrow{EF}$? ....

    iii) $\overrightarrow{AB}$ and $\overrightarrow{GH}$? ....

    iv) $\overrightarrow{AB}$ and $\overrightarrow{OP}$? ....

c) Complete the following. Give your answers in the form $\begin{pmatrix} x \\ y \end{pmatrix}$.

    i) $\overrightarrow{AB} + \overrightarrow{CD}$ **ii)** $\overrightarrow{AB} - \overrightarrow{CD}$

    iii) $\overrightarrow{HG} + \overrightarrow{EF}$ **iv)** $\overrightarrow{HG} - \overrightarrow{GH}$

    v) $\overrightarrow{IJ} + \overrightarrow{OP}$ **vi)** $2\overrightarrow{KL} + \overrightarrow{GH}$

    vii) $\overrightarrow{IJ} + \overrightarrow{MN}$ **viii)** $\frac{1}{2}\overrightarrow{GH} - \overrightarrow{KL}$

    ix) $\overrightarrow{OP} - \overrightarrow{PO}$ **x)** $\overrightarrow{AB} + \overrightarrow{CD} + \overrightarrow{MN}$

2 The diagram below shows three vectors a, b and c.

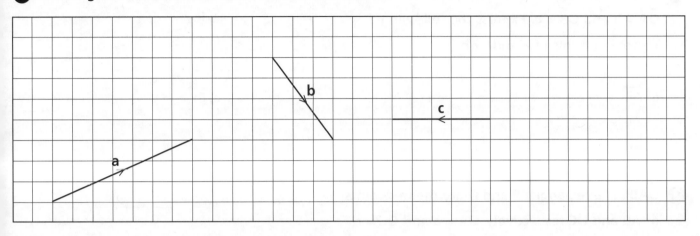

On the grid below, draw and label diagrams to represent...

a) a + b   b) a - b   c) b + c   d) b - c   e) 2a - c   f) a - 3c

3 If a = $\begin{pmatrix} 3 \\ 4 \end{pmatrix}$, b = $\begin{pmatrix} 2 \\ 3 \end{pmatrix}$, c = $\begin{pmatrix} -4 \\ -3 \end{pmatrix}$ and d = $\begin{pmatrix} 4 \\ -1 \end{pmatrix}$, on a suitable grid draw diagrams to represent...

a) 2a   b) 2c   c) a + b   d) a + c   e) b + c   f) b - c   g) c - d   h) c + 2d

Vector Geometry

1 OAB is a triangle. P is the midpoint of OA.
$\overrightarrow{OA}$ = a and $\overrightarrow{OB}$ = b. Express the following
vectors in terms of a and/or b:

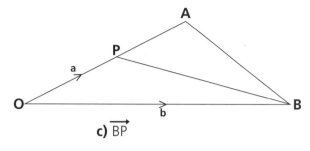

a) $\overrightarrow{AB}$

b) $\overrightarrow{PA}$

c) $\overrightarrow{BP}$

....

....

2 OABC is a rectangle. P and Q are the midpoints
of AB and OC respectively. $\overrightarrow{OA}$ = a and $\overrightarrow{OC}$ = c.

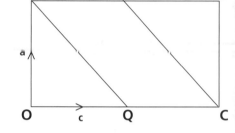

a) Express the following vectors in terms of **a** and/or **c**.

   i) $\overrightarrow{CB}$ ....   **ii)** $\overrightarrow{AB}$ ....

   iii) $\overrightarrow{PB}$ ....   **iv)** $\overrightarrow{OQ}$ ....

   v) $\overrightarrow{PC}$ ....

   vi) $\overrightarrow{AQ}$ ....

b) What can you deduce about shape APCQ? Explain your answer.

....

....

3 OABC is a parallelogram. P is a point on OA so that OP = $\frac{1}{3}$OA,
Q is a point on OC so that OQ = $\frac{1}{3}$OC, X is a point on AB so
that AX = $\frac{1}{3}$ AB and Y is a point on CB so that CY = $\frac{1}{3}$CB.
$\overrightarrow{OA}$ = a and $\overrightarrow{OC}$ = c.

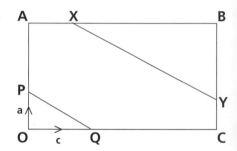

a) Express the following vectors in terms of **a** and/or **c**:

   i) $\overrightarrow{OP}$ ....   **ii)** $\overrightarrow{OQ}$ ....

   iii) $\overrightarrow{PQ}$ ....   **iv)** $\overrightarrow{BX}$ ....

   v) $\overrightarrow{BY}$ ....   **vi)** $\overrightarrow{XY}$ ....

b) What can you deduce about shape PXYQ? Explain your answer.

....

....

....

4 P, Q, R and S are the midpoints of sides AB, BC, CD and DA of parallelogram ABCD respectively. Prove that
PQRS is also a parallelogram.

5 G and H are the midpoints of sides AB and AC of triangle ABC respectively.
   a) Prove that triangle AGH and ABC are similar.
   b) What is the ratio of the two triangles' areas?

Perimeter

1 Calculate the perimeter of the following shapes. Where lengths are not given, use a ruler to measure the sides.

a)

....

....

b)

....

....

c)

....

....

d)

....

....

e)

....

....

f)

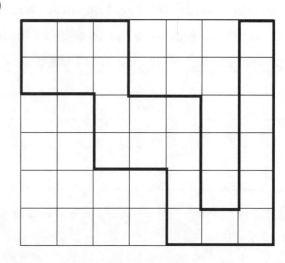

....

....

Circumference of a Circle

1 A window is in the shape of a semicircle on top of a rectangle, as shown in the diagram. If AB = 1.8m and BC = 90cm, calculate the perimeter of the window to 1 decimal place. Take π = 3.14.

....

....

....

....

2 Mrs Jones' garden is rectangular. At each end there is a semicircular flower bed and the rest of the garden is lawn, as shown in the diagram. If AB = 10m and BC = 8m, calculate the perimeter of the lawn. Take π = 3.14

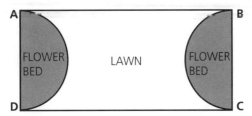

....

....

....

....

3 Christmas decorations are made using the template shown. Ribbon is sewn around the outside edge of each decoration. How much ribbon is needed to make 15 decorations? Take π = 3.14

....

....

....

....

4 The minor sector OXY is cut out of a circle and the two radii OX and OY are joined edge to edge to form a cone as shown opposite. Calculate the radius of the base of the cone.

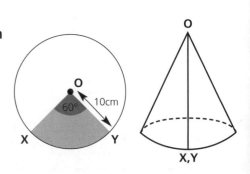

....

....

....

....

5 Calculate the circumference of the following circles to 1 decimal place. Take π = 3.14
a) Radius = 12cm **b)** Radius = 1.2cm **c)** Diameter = 12cm **d)** Diameter = 120cm

6 Sector OAB (shaded) is cut out of a circle with a radius of 16cm.
a) Calculate the perimeter of sector OAB.
b) Calculate the perimeter of the major sector left over.

1 Estimate the area of the following shapes. Each square has an area of 1cm².

a)

b)

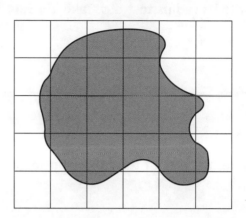

....

2 Calculate the area of the following shapes. They are not drawn to scale. Take π = 3.14

a)

6cm

6cm

....

....

b)

90cm

1.2m

....

....

c)

7.5cm

10cm

....

....

d)

6.4cm

10cm

....

....

e)

15cm

2.4cm

....

....

f)

19cm

12cm

25cm

....

....

g)

62cm

0.5m

80cm

....

....

h)

10cm

....

....

i)

10cm

....

....

Area 1 & 2 (cont)

3 A circular table has an area of 11.304m².
Calculate its radius to 1 d.p. Take π = 3.14

....
....
....
....

4 A circular flower bed has an area of 7.065m².
Calculate its radius to 1 d.p. Take π = 3.14

....
....
....
....

5 Calculate the area of the following shapes to 1 d.p. They are not drawn to scale. Take π = 3.14

a)

b)

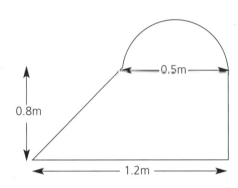

....
....
....
....
....

....
....
....
....
....

6 Mrs Jones' garden is rectangular. At each end there is a semi-circular flower bed and the rest of the garden is lawn. If AB = 10m and BC = 8m, calculate the area of the lawn. Take π = 3.14

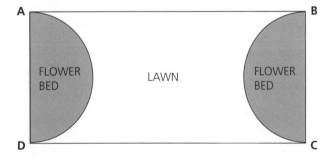

....
....
....
....
....
....
....

7 A property developer decides to varnish the floorboards in the living room of one of his houses. A plan of the floor is shown alongside. It is not to scale. One tin of varnish will cover 16m² and costs £4.99. If he wants to apply two coats of varnish to the whole floor, how much will it cost him?

6 Calculate the areas of these triangles to 2 decimal places.

a)

8cm

58°

7.5cm

b)

7.3cm

6.4cm   45°

c)

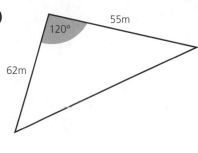

55m

120°

62m

....
....
....
....

....
....
....
....

....
....
....
....

7 The diagram opposite shows a field. Calculate its area.

....
....
....
....
....
....

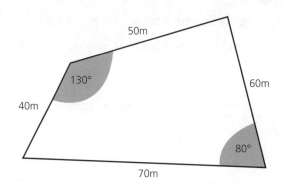

50m

130°

40m

60m

80°

70m

8

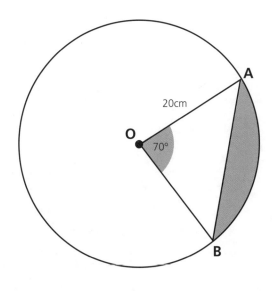

A

20cm

O

70°

B

a) Calculate the area of triangle OAB to 2 decimal places.

....
....
....
....

b) Calculate the area of sector OAB. Hence, find the area of the shaded segment to 2 decimal places.

....
....
....
....

9 Calculate the area of the following triangles:
 a) Triangle ABC has AB = 38cm, BC = 25cm and $A\widehat{B}C$ = 58°.
 b) Triangle ABC has AB = 20cm, BC = 5cm and $A\widehat{B}C$ = 100°.

Area 3 & 4

1 Calculate the surface area of the following solids to 1 d.p.

a)

b)

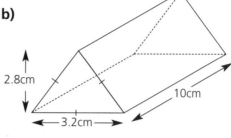

....

....

....

....

....

....

....

....

2 The outside of a cylindrical drum is painted. The drum has a radius of 5cm and a height of 12cm. π = 3.14 Find the total surface area of the drum including both ends to 3 s.f.

....

....

....

....

3 A child's night light is spherical in shape, with radius 4cm. Calculate the surface area of the light to 3 s.f. (π = 3.14).

....

....

4 Calculate the total surface area of the cone-shaped tent opposite. Take π = 3.14

....

....

....

5 Using π = 3.14, calculate the surface area of a sphere with...
a) radius 7cm b) radius 3.7cm c) diameter 10cm d) diameter 28cm.

6 Calculate the surface area of the shape shown, which is half a sphere on top of a cone. Take π = 3.14

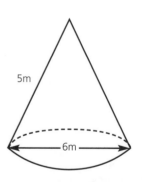

1 Calculate the volume of the following solids.

a)

b)

$\pi = 3.14$

c)

....
....
....
....

2 **a)** The following cylinder has a volume of 314cm³.
Calculate the missing length represented by x
($\pi = 3.14$).

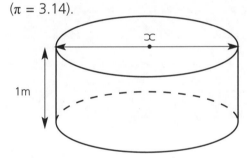

b) The following solid has a volume of 100cm³.
Calculate the missing length represented by x.

....
....
....
....

3 **A globe has a diameter of 30cm. Take $\pi = 3.14$**
Calculate its volume to 3 s.f.

....
....
....
....
....
....
....

Volume 1, 2 & 3 (cont)

4 A firework has a conical shape with a base radius of 2cm and a height of 7.5cm. Calculate its volume.

....

....

....

....

....

....

5 The tank opposite contains water. The depth of the water is 50cm. All the water is poured into a cylindrical tank which has a diameter of 44cm. Calculate the depth of the water in the cylindrical tank (to 1d.p.) $\pi = 3.14$

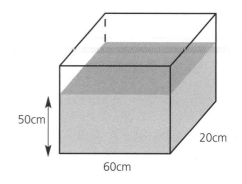

....

....

....

....

....

6 In the following expressions the letters r and h represent length. π, 2, 3, 4, 5, and 10 are numbers which have no dimension. Write down whether each of the following expressions represent perimeter, area, volume or none of them.

a) $r(\pi + 2)$ ....

b) $\dfrac{4r^2\pi}{h}$ ....

c) $r(r + 4h)$ ....

d) $\dfrac{rh}{4}$ ....

e) $10r^3\pi$ ....

f) $\pi(r + 2h)$ ....

g) $\dfrac{3r^3}{h}$ ....

h) $r^2(h + \pi r)$ ....

7 A cylindrical mug has internal radius 5cm and internal height 8cm.
   a) Calculate the volume of liquid it can hold (to 3 sig. fig.) ($\pi = 3.14$)
   b) If 500cm^3 of liquid is poured into the mug, what would the depth of liquid be in the mug?

8 If x and y both represent length, which of the following expressions represent **i)** length, **ii)** area, **iii)** volume?
   $\dfrac{x}{y}$, $\sqrt{x^3}$, $x^2 + y^2$, $\dfrac{x^2}{y}$, xy^2, x^2y^2, $x^2 + y^3$

Similar Figures

1 Two figures are similar. The ratio of two corresponding lengths is 2:3.

    a) What is the ratio of their areas? ....

    b) What is the ratio of their volumes? ....

2 Two figures are similar. The ratio of their areas is 6.25:16. What is the ratio of their volumes?

....

....

3 The diagram shows two similar figures. The height of Figure A is 12cm and the height of Figure B is 27cm.

Figure B   27cm

Figure A   12cm

    a) If the surface area of Figure A is 72cm², calculate the surface area of Figure B.

....

....

....

....

....

    b) If the volume of Figure B is 243cm³, calculate the volume of Figure A.

....

....

....

....

....

4 Two figures are similar. The volume of Figure A is 108cm³ and the volume of Figure B is 500cm³. If the surface area of Figure B is 60cm², what is the surface area of Figure A?

....

....

....

5 Two figures are similar. The surface area of Figure A is 150cm² and the surface area of Figure B is 294cm². If the volume of Figure A is 275cm³, what is the volume of Figure B?

....

....

....

6 Three bottles are similar. Bottle A has a height of 6cm, a surface area of 12cm² and a volume of 9cm³.

    a) If Bottle B has a surface area of 75cm², calculate **i)** its height and **ii)** its volume.

    b) If Bottle C has a volume of 72cm³, calculate **i)** its height and **ii)** its surface area.

7 Is it possible for Figure A, which has a height of 22cm and a volume of 135cm³, to be similar to Figure B, which has a height of 33cm and a volume of 320cm³? Explain.

3-D Shapes 1 & 2

1 **a)** What shape is the base of the cuboid shown opposite? ....

b) Which edges are equal in length to CD? ....

c) Which lengths equal AH? ....

d) How many vertices has the cuboid? ....

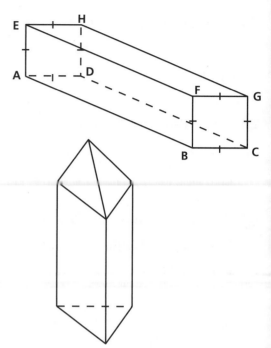

2 **An equilateral triangular prism has a tetrahedron placed on top of it. For this combined solid...**

a) How many edges does it have? ....

b) How many vertices? ....

c) How many faces? ....

3 **On the grid below draw full scale diagrams of the following solids:**

a)

2cm
2cm
3cm

b)

1cm
1cm
1cm
2cm
2cm
3cm

4 **Draw a sketch of the plan view of this square-based pyramid.**

3-D Shapes 1 & 2 (cont)

5 The diagram alongside shows a solid. Draw and label an accurate diagram of the solid showing...

a) plan view b) front elevation c) side elevation

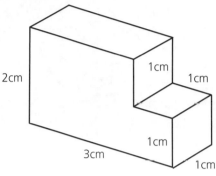

6 A net of a solid is shown opposite.

a) What is the name of the 3-D solid?

....

b) How many vertices does it have?

....

c) Which other corners meet at D? Put an X on each one.

d) How many planes of symmetry does the solid have?

....

7 Which of the following are nets for a triangular prism? Place a tick beside the correct net(s).

a)

b)

c)

d)

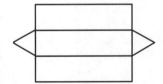

8 Draw an accurate full-size net of a regular hexagonal prism if each edge is 3cm long.

9 How many planes of symmetry does a cube have?

10 Draw the a) plan b) front elevation c) side elevation of this solid.

Symmetry 1 & 2

1 Draw all the lines of symmetry for each of the following shapes.

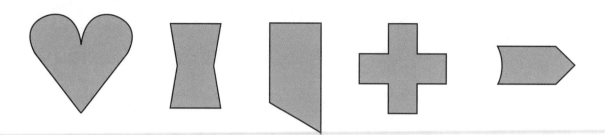

2 Mark on the lines of symmetry for each of these letters.

M S H B Z A V C K

3 How many lines of symmetry do each of the following quadrilaterals have?

a) Square .... ☐

b) Rectangle .... ▭

c) Parallelogram .... ▱

d) Rhombus .... ▱

e) Kite ....◁

f) Trapezium ....◺

4 For each of the following shapes draw in all the lines of symmetry and also write down the order of rotational symmetry for each shape.

a)

b)

c)

Order of rotational symmetry:

....

Order of rotational symmetry:

....

Order of rotational symmetry:

....

5 What is the order of rotational symmetry for each of these letters?

X   H   I   Z   K   S   E   N

....

6 What is the order of rotational symmetry for each of these shapes?

a)   b)   c)   d)

Order:..............................   Order:..............................   Order:..............................   Order:..............................

7 **a)** Draw accurately a regular pentagon with sides 3cm long and interior angles 108°.

b) Mark on the lines of symmetry.

c) What is the order of rotational symmetry?

....

8 **a)** Draw a regular hexagon. Interior angles are 120°.
     b) Draw in all lines of symmetry and write down the order of rotational symmetry.

9 Write down the order of rotational symmetry for each quadrilateral:
     a) Square **b)** Rectangle **c)** Parallelogram **d)** Rhombus **e)** Kite **f)** Trapezium.

Scale Drawings & Map Scales

1 a) Draw an accurate scale drawing of this garden, using a scale of 1cm to represent 2.5m.

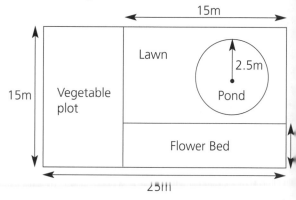

b) What is the actual diagonal distance across the garden in metres?

....

2 This is part of a map of Devon and Cornwall drawn to a scale of 1cm : 10km.

a) What is the direct distance from Launceston to Exeter?

....

....

b) What is the direct distance between Bodmin and Looe?

....

....

c) Name two places that are a direct distance of 43km from Tavistock

....

....

3 Draw an accurate scale drawing of a rectangular field 80m long and 50m wide. By measurement, find the actual distance diagonally from one corner to the opposite corner, to the nearest metre.

4 The diagram alongside shows a sketch of one side of a house.
a) Draw an accurate scale drawing using a scale of 1cm to 1m.
b) By measurement, find the actual height of the house (x).

Measuring Bearings

1 The diagram shows the position of the coastguard (C), the beach (B) and a yacht (Y).

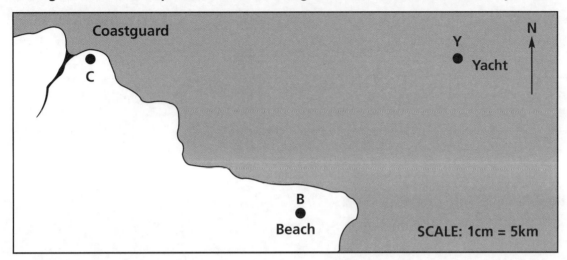

a) What is the bearing of…

i) Y from C? .... **ii)** Y from B? ....

iii) B from C? .... **iv)** B from Y? ....

v) C from Y? .... **vi)** C from B? ....

b) What is the actual distance from…

i) C to B? .... **ii)** C to Y? .... **iii)** B to Y? ....

2 The map shows the position of 4 towns A, B, C and D on an island. A helicopter flies directly from A to B, then B to C, then C to D and finally D back to A. On what four bearings must it fly?

A ➤ B ....

B ➤ C ....

C ➤ D ....

D ➤ A ....

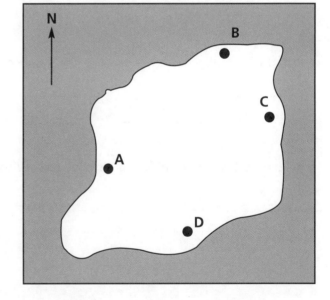

3 An explorer walks 1000m on a bearing of 070° and then walks 2000m on a bearing of 160°.

a) Draw an accurate scale drawing of his route.

b) By measurement, find the bearing he must follow to return directly to his starting point.

4 Treasure is buried on an island according to the following instructions: "The treasure lies on a bearing of 100° from the coconut tree and on a bearing of 200° from the cactus plant. The cactus plant is 20m due east of the coconut tree." Draw a scale drawing using 1cm to 5m to show the position of the treasure.

Converting Measurements

1 **Convert...**

   a) 450cm into metres

   ....

   ....

   d) 6874g into kg

   ....

   ....

   b) 3.5 litres into millilitres

   ....

   ....

   e) 45km into metres

   ....

   ....

   c) 1.25kg into grams

   ....

   ....

   f) 0.55cm into mm

   ....

   ....

2 **Convert these lengths into metres.**

   a) 1005cm

   ....

   ....

   b) 1.937km

   ....

   ....

   c) 2650mm

   ....

   ....

3 **Put these weights into order of size, smallest first.**

   420g, 4kg, 39.5kg, 4220mg, 0.405kg

   ....

   ....

   ....

4 **Convert...**

   a) 45cm into inches

   ....

   ....

   b) 6 ounces into grams

   ....

   ....

   c) 5 gallons into litres

   ....

   ....

5 **Terry is 1.5m tall. Jake is 68 inches tall. Who is taller and by how much?**

   ....

   ....

   ....

6 **Put these lengths into decreasing order of size:**
1km, 900m, 1200m, 11 000cm, 1 050 000mm

7 **Convert...**
a) 3 miles into km   **b)** 12km into miles   **c)** 4.5 pounds into grams   **d)** 360g into pounds   **e)** 12 pints into litres
f) 22.5 litres into pints

8 **Sue ran a 10km race. How many yards did she run altogether? (1760 yards = 1 mile).**

Compound Measures

1 Work out the time taken to travel 92km at an average speed of 55km/h.

....

....

2 A marathon runner completed 26.2 miles in a course record of 2hrs 20mins.
What was his average speed?

....

....

3 A tortoise took 20 minutes to get from one end of the garden to the other. His average speed is
2cm per second. How long is the garden in metres?

....

....

....

4 A boat travels for $2\frac{1}{2}$ hours at 100km/h and then $1\frac{1}{2}$ hours at 80km/h. Calculate its average speed
for the whole journey.

....

....

....

5 A cylindrical tree stump weighs 15kg.
Its dimensions are shown opposite.
Calculate the density of the wood.

....

....

....

50cm

30cm

6 Water has a density of 1g/cm^3 and ice has a density of 0.9g/cm^3.
450cm^3 of water is frozen. By how much does the volume of the water change when it freezes?

....

....

....

7 a) Change 30 metres per second into km per hour.
b) A car travels 30 metres per second for $3\frac{1}{2}$ hours. How far does it travel in km?

8 The density of oak wood is 800kg per m^3.
a) Change this to g per cm^3.
b) How much does a solid oak table top measuring 110cm by 80cm by 5cm weigh?

Constructions 1 & 2

1 Construct a triangle ABC with sides AB = 4cm, BC = 3cm and angle $A\hat{B}C$ = 40°.

2 On your triangle ABC in question 1 above, construct the bisector of angle $B\hat{A}C$.

3 **a)** Construct a triangle PQR where PQ is 6cm, QR is 5cm and PR is 2cm.

b) Construct the perpendicular bisector of PQ and where this line meets QR, label it S.

4 The sketch opposite shows three towns A, B and C. B is on a bearing of 040° from A. C is due East of A and B is on a bearing of 300° from C. C is 40km from A. Construct an accurate scale drawing.

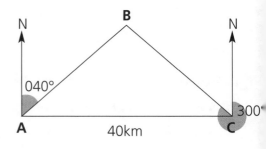

5 Showing all construction lines, and by using a pair of compasses and a ruler, construct the perpendicular bisector of each side of this equilateral triangle.

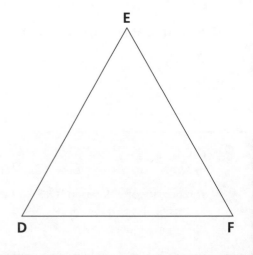

6 **Using the line AB below as a starting point, use a pair of compasses and a ruler to...**

a) Construct a 90° angle at A

b) Construct a 90° angle at B

c) Complete the construction to make a square.

You must show all of your construction lines.

A   B

7 **In the space below draw a triangle XYZ.**

a) Construct the bisectors of the three angles $\hat{X}$, $\hat{Y}$ and $\hat{Z}$. You must show all of your construction lines.

b) What do you notice? ....

8 **Using only a ruler and a pair of compasses, construct...**
a) an equilateral triangle of side 3cm
b) a square of side 6cm.

9 **Construct the following triangles using a ruler and a pair of compasses.**

a)

7.4cm   5.3cm

5.3cm

b)

6.2cm

60°

7.3cm

c)

8.4cm

60°

9cm

d)

5.5cm

6.5cm

Loci

1 The points B, C and D represent three schools Biggley, Chiggley and Diggley. Pupils are entitled to a free bus pass if they live within 5km of the school they attend. Some pupils would be entitled to a free bus pass to all three schools. Drawn an accurate diagram to show the region in which these pupils live.

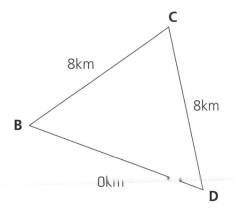

2 A goat is tethered by a rope 4m long to a rail PQ 8m long. The rope can move along the rail from P to Q. Draw an accurate diagram of the locus of points showing the area where the goat can eat grass.

3 Draw a triangle ABC where AB = 7cm, BC = 9cm, AB̂C = 90°.
   a) Draw the locus of points inside the triangle which are equidistant from A and B.
   b) Draw the locus of points inside the triangle which are equidistant from B and C.
   c) Find and label a point D which is equidistant from A and B and equidistant from B and C.

4 Draw the same triangle ABC as for question 3.
   a) Draw the locus of points equidistant from line AB and AC.
   b) A point (P) moves inside triangle ABC, equidistant from AB and AC and greater than 6cm away from C.
   Show the locus of points where P can move.

Properties of Circles 1 & 2

1 Name each of the parts of the circle labelled A to F opposite.

a) A .... **b)** B ....

c) C .... **d)** D ....

e) E .... **f)** F ....

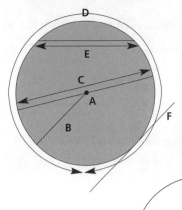

2 In the diagram opposite, O is the centre of the circle. AB is a tangent touching the circle at C. OC = AC. Find the size of...

a) angle CÔA ....

b) angle OD̂C ....

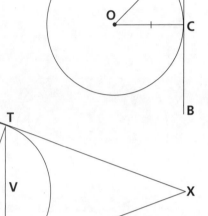

3 XT and XW are tangents touching the circle at T and W.

a) Draw the axis of symmetry in OTXW.

b) Name three pairs of congruent triangles.

....

c) If angle TX̂W is 40° what is angle TÔW?

....

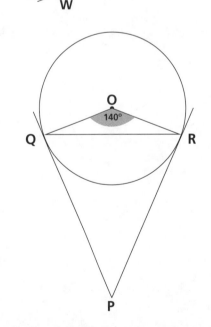

4 In the diagram opposite, O is the centre of the circle and PQ and PR are tangents.

a) What name is given to triangle OQR? ....

b) Find the size of angle...

i) OQ̂R ....

ii) OR̂Q ....

c) Find the size of angle...

i) RQ̂P ....

ii) QR̂P ....

iii) QP̂R ....

d) What type of triangle is PQR? ....

5 **a)** In diagram A calculate the length OX if the chord is 10m long and radius OW is 8m long.

   b) In diagram B, AB and CD are parallel chords. OPQ is perpendicular to AB and CD. Explain why AC = BD.

Diagram A

Diagram B

Properties of Circles 3 & 4

1 Find the size of x. Give a reason for your answer. They are not drawn to scale.

a)

....
....

b)

....
....

c)

....
....

d)

....
....

e)

....
....

f)

....
....

g)

....
....

h)

....
....

i)

....
....

j)

....
....

k)

....
....

l)

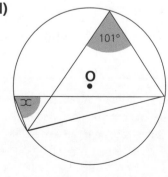

....
....

Properties of Circles 3 & 4 (cont)

2 Find the size of x and y. Give a reason for your answer. They are not drawn to scale.

a)

b)

c)

....

....

....

....

....

....

3 Find the size of angle AED. Give a reason for your answer. They are not drawn to scale.

a)

b)

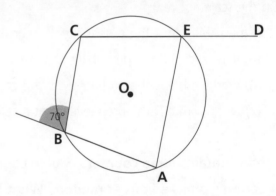

....

....

....

....

4 Calculate the value of x. They are not drawn to scale.

a)

b)

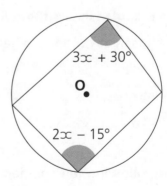

....

....

....

....

5 By means of a suitable diagram prove the following:
a) The angle subtended by a semicircle is 90°   b) Opposite angles of a cyclic quadrilateral add up to 180°.
c) The angle subtended between a tangent to a circle and its chord is equal to the angle subtended in the alternate segment.   d) Angles subtended by an arc are equal in size.   e) Angles subtended in the same segment are equal in size.

Probability 1 & 2

1 Tim has ten cards (shown below). They are placed face down and mixed up.

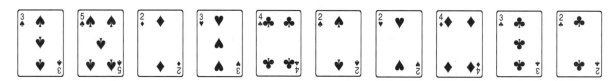

a) What is the probability that a card picked at random will be…

i) a 2? ....

ii) a 3? ....

iii) a 4? ....

iv) a 5? ....

v) not a 2? ....

vi) not a 3? ....

b) Here is a probability scale:

0.5

0   1

On the scale above…

i) mark with an A the probability that a card picked at random will be a 2.

ii) mark with a B the probability that a card picked at random will be a 3.

iii) mark with a C the probability that a card picked at random will be a 4.

iv) mark with a D the probability that a card picked at random will be a 5.

2 A bag contains 4 red counters, 5 blue counters and 9 yellow counters.

A counter is picked out at random. What is the probability that it is…

a) red? ....

b) not red? ....

c) blue? ....

d) not blue? ....

e) yellow? ....

f) not yellow? ....

3 A page in a calendar shows the following month of June.

If a date is chosen at random. What is the probability that it is…

a) an even number? ....

b) an odd number? ....

c) a prime number? ....

d) a weekday? ....

e) not a weekday? ....

JUNE

S	M	T	W	T	F	S
			1	2	3	4	5
6	7	8	9	10	11	12
13	14	15	16	17	18	19
20	21	22	23	24	25	26
27	28	29	30			

4 Jack has the following fair spinner. He spins it.

a) What is the probability that the spinner does not land on a 1?

....

b) What is the probability that the spinner does not land on a 2?

....

c) What is the probability that the spinner lands on a 3?

....

5 Vicky has two sets of cards, A and B as shown below:

A   B

a) Complete all the possible outcomes if two cards are picked, one from A and one from B, at random.

b) What is the probability that the two cards picked are **i)** both 2s? ....

   ii) both the same suit? .... **iii)** not the same suit?.................................

6 Brian's pencil case contains blue, black, red and green biros only. The probability of picking out a biro of a certain colour is shown in the table. What is the probability that the biro picked out is red?

Colour of biro	Probability of picking that colour
Blue	0.2
Black	0.35
Red	....
Green	0.15

7 On her way to work, Safia has to drive through a set of traffic lights. The probability that Safia will arrive at work on time is 0.4 and that she will arrive late is 0.25 What is the probability that she will arrive early?

....

8 A bag contains 8 blue marbles, 6 red marbles and 2 green marbles. One marble is pulled out at random and not replaced back into the bag. A second marble is then picked out at random.

a) What is the probability that the second marble picked out is blue, if the first marble picked out was green? ....

b) What is the probability that the second marble picked out is green, if the first marble picked out was also green? ....

9 A box contains 7 red balls and 3 blue balls. A ball is picked out at random.
What is the probability that it is **a)** red? **b)** not red? **c)** blue? **d)** not blue? **e)** red or blue? **f)** black?

10 A kitchen cupboard contains tins of baked beans, peas, carrots and potatoes only. The probability of picking a tin of potatoes is $\frac{1}{12}$, while the probability of picking a tin of carrots is three times that of a tin of potatoes, and a tin of peas is twice that of a tin of carrots.
a) What is the probability of picking **i)** a tin of carrots? **ii)** a tin of peas? **iii)** a tin of baked beans?
b) What is the probability of not picking **i)** a tin of carrots? **ii)** a tin of peas? **iii)** a tin of baked beans?
c) If the cupboard contains 4 tins of baked beans, how many tins are there in the cupboard altogether?

Probability 3

1 There are a number of red, white and blue beads in a bag. The probability of picking a red bead is $\frac{1}{3}$ and the probability of picking a blue bead is $\frac{1}{5}$.

a) What is the probability of picking a red or blue bead?

....

b) What is the probability of picking a white or red bead?

....

....

2 There are 52 cards in a pack. One is picked at random. What is the probability that it is...

a) a heart or a diamond? ....

b) a heart or a king? (Careful!) ....

3 If two fair dice are thrown, what is the probability of the results being...

a) two sixes? ....

b) two odd numbers? ....

4 There are 10 discs in a bag of which 3 are blue. Two discs are picked out at random without being replaced. What is the probability of getting two blue discs?

....

....

5 Vicky has a set of five cards, shown below. They are placed face down. She also has an ordinary fair die.

A card is picked at random and the die is thrown.

a) What is the probability of throwing a 3 or 4 with the die and picking up a card with a 2 on it?

....

b) What is the probability of throwing an odd number with the die and picking a card with an odd number on it?

....

6 A box contains 3 blue, 4 yellow, 5 red and 2 green sweets. One is taken out and eaten. A second is then taken out. What is the probability that...
  a) both sweets are green?
  b) both sweets are the same colour?

Listing All Outcomes

1 **Two fair dice are thrown and the two numbers are added together to give a total score.**

a) Complete the sample space diagram below to show all the scores:

First Die						
+	**1**	**2**	**3**	**4**	**5**	**6**
1	2	3	4			
2	3	4				
3	4					
4						
5						
6						

Second Die (row label)

b) What is the probability that the total score will be...

i) equal to 7? ....

ii) greater than 7? ....

iii) a prime number? ....

iv) a square number? ....

v) greater than 12? ....

vi) a multiple of 3? ....

vii) a factor of 12? ....

2 **Francis has the following coins in her pocket:**

Jim has the following coins in his pocket:

Two coins are picked out at random, one from Francis' pocket and one from Jim's pocket.
The values of the two coins are added together.

a) Complete the sample space diagram below to show all the values:

Francis' Coin					

Jim's Coin (row label)

b) What is the probability that the total value of the two coins added together is...

i) equal to 6p? ....

ii) equal to 11p? ....

iii) less than 10p? ....

iv) greater than 40p? ....

v) less than 40p? ....

vi) equal to 40p? ....

3 Bruce has an ordinary fair die. Robin has the fair spinner shown alongside:
The spinner is spun and the die is thrown to give two numbers.
a) Draw a sample space diagram to show all the possible scores if the numbers are multiplied together.
b) What is the probability that the score is **i)** equal to 12? **ii)** equal to 24? **iii)** a multiple of 10?
iv) a factor of 4? **v)** an odd number? **vi)** an even number?

Tree Diagrams 1 & 2

1 The probability that Steve arrives at school on time on any particular day is 0.7

a) Complete the tree diagram for two school days, Monday and Tuesday.

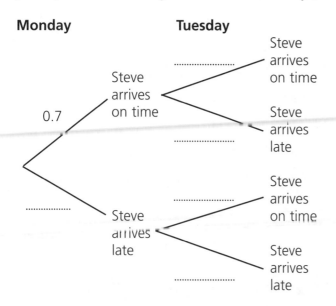

Monday **Tuesday**

0.7 — Steve arrives on time
Steve arrives on time
Steve arrives late

Steve arrives late
Steve arrives on time
Steve arrives late

b) What is the probability that…

i) Steve arrives on time on Monday and Tuesday?

....

ii) Steve arrives late on Monday and Tuesday?

....

iii) Steve arrives late on Monday only?

....

iv) Steve arrives late on Tuesday only?

....

v) Steve arrives late on one day only?

....

2 Vicky, Donna and Petra are going to have two races. The probability that Vicky wins either of the two races is 0.5, while the probability that Donna wins either of the two races is 0.3.

a) What is the probability of Petra winning either of the two races? ....

b) Complete the tree diagram.

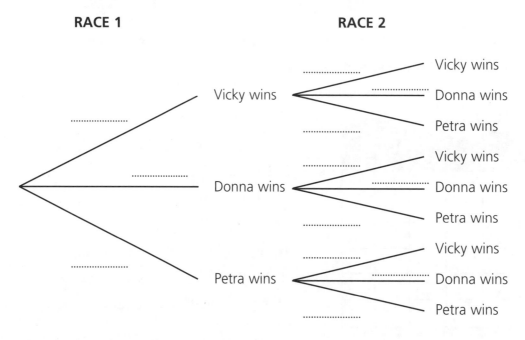

RACE 1 **RACE 2**

Vicky wins
— Vicky wins
— Donna wins
— Petra wins

Donna wins
— Vicky wins
— Donna wins
— Petra wins

Petra wins
— Vicky wins
— Donna wins
— Petra wins

c) What is the probability that…

i) Vicky wins both races? ....

ii) Vicky does not win a race? ....

iii) Donna wins Race 1 and Petra wins Race 2? ....

iv) Race 1 and Race 2 are won by different girls? ....

Tree Diagrams 1 & 2 (cont)

3 **A bag contains 12 counters of which 6 are black, 4 are white and 2 are red. A counter is picked out at random and, without it being replaced, another counter is picked out at random.**

a) In the space below draw a tree diagram to show all the different possible outcomes.

b) What is the probability that…

i) Both counters picked out are the same colour? ....

ii) Both counters picked out are different colours? ....

iii) Neither of the counters picked out are black? ....

---

4 **The probability that Julie does her school homework on any particular day is 0.8.**
a) Draw a tree diagram to show all the probabilities for two days.
b) Using the tree diagram, what is the probability that Julie **i)** does her homework on both days **ii)** does her homework on one day only and **iii)** does not do her homework on either day?

5 **Rolf is a cricketer. The probability that Rolf's team win a game is $\frac{1}{2}$ and lose is $\frac{1}{3}$. They can also draw. Rolf's team have a cricket game on Saturday and another game on Sunday.**
a) Draw a tree diagram to show all the probabilities. **b)** Using the tree diagram, what is the probability that Rolf's team **i)** win both games **ii)** win on Saturday only **iii)** win one game only **iv)** do not lose either game?

6 **A bag contains 12 balls of which 4 are red, 3 are blue, 3 are green and 2 are yellow. A ball is picked at random and, without it being replaced, another ball is picked at random.**
a) Draw a tree diagram to show all the different possible outcomes.
b) What is the probability that **i)** both balls are the same colour **ii)** both balls are different colours **iii)** neither of the balls picked out are red?

Relative Frequency

1 **The following fair spinner is spun 120 times:**

a) How many times would you expect the spinner to land on…

i) a 1?... **ii)** a 2?... **iii)** a 3?...

b) The actual number of times the spinner landed on a 1, 2 and 3 is shown in the table below. For each number calculate the relative frequency.

Number	Number of times landed	Relative Frequency
1	66	....
2	38	....
3	16	....

2 **Jane tosses a coin 50, 100, 150, 200 and 250 times. She records the number of tails she gets in a table (shown alongside):**

Number of tosses	Number of tails	Relative Frequency
50	20	0.4
100	44	....
150	80	....
200	92	....
250	120	....

a) Complete the table by calculating the missing relative frequencies.

b) On the grid below draw a bar graph to show the relative frequency of the coin landing on tails.

c) If Jane kept tossing the coin, what would you expect the relative frequency of the coin landing on tails to become? Explain why.

....

....

....

....

....

3 **Below are the results of an experiment where a die was thrown and the number of sixes was recorded.**

Number of throws	30	60	90	120	150	180	210	240	270	300	330	360
Number of sixes thrown	3	5	10	16	23	28	35	42	47	49	52	59
Relative frequency												

a) Complete the table by calculating the missing relative frequencies.
b) Draw a bar graph to show the relative frequency of throwing a 6.
c) How many 6s would you expect to be thrown if the experiment was continued and the die was thrown 1500 times?

Collecting Data 1 & 2

1 **What is the difference between primary data and secondary data?**

....

....

....

2 **a)** What is sampling?

....

b) What is the difference between a random sample and a stratified sample?

....

....

c) A recent survey carried out in Manchester suggests that 90% of the national population prefer football to rugby. The survey was conducted on 200 males. Has this survey provided reliable data? Explain why.

....

....

....

3 **Jenny is concerned about the breakfast habits of the pupils at her school. She decides to use a questionnaire to find out what pupils have to eat for breakfast. She has chosen eight questions for her questionnaire. Decide whether each question is suitable or not suitable, giving a reason for your answer.**

a) Everybody should eat breakfast. Don't you agree?

....

b) Do you eat breakfast?

....

c) What time do you get up in the morning?

....

d) Are you a vegetarian?

....

e) What year are you in?

....

f) What do you have to eat if you have breakfast?

....

g) If you eat breakfast do you have cereal, toast or other?

....

h) Do you brush your teeth before breakfast?

....

Collecting Data 1 & 2 (cont)

4 **Joe works in a supermarket. He decides to use a questionnaire to find out about the shopping habits of the customers who come into the store. Here is the first question:**

'How old are you?' Tick the correct box

Under 10 years		11 years to 20 years		21 years to 40 years		41 years to 60 years		61 years to 80 years		Over 80 years	

a) Make up two more suitable questions Joe could use for his questionnaire.

....

....

b) Make up two questions which would not be suitable for his questionnaire.

....

....

5 **In a survey a group of pupils were asked, 'How long did you spend watching TV over the weekend?'**

a) Design a suitable observation sheet to collect this information.

b) How would you make sure that the information obtained was from a random sample?

....

....

6 **Molly works in a pizza parlour. She decides to use a questionnaire to find out about the eating habits of the people who come into the parlour.**
a) Make up three suitable questions Molly could use for her questionnaire.
b) Make up three questions which are not suitable for her questionnaire.

7 **Jimmy is carrying out a survey to investigate what the pupils in his school spend their pocket money on.**
a) Design a suitable observation sheet for him to collect the information.
b) How could Jimmy make sure that the information collected was random.

1 What is the difference between discrete and continuous data?

....

....

....

....

2 Jane is carrying out a traffic survey. She records the number of cars that pass her house every 30 seconds for a period of 20 minutes. Group her data by completing the frequency table below.

Number of cars
4 3 4 ~~4~~ 2 5 5 4 3 2
4 5 3 2 4 4 4 5 5 ~~5~~
2 4 3 5 4 3 3 5 2 4
2 4 3 5 2 ~~5~~ ~~5~~ 4 5 3

Number of cars	Tally	Frequency
1	IIII	4
2		
3		
4		
5		

3 A survey was carried out on the number of residents in each house on a street.

The results are given below:

4, 5, 3, 4, 3, 6, 1, 5, 4, 2, 3, 4, 5, 2, 4, 5, 5, 3, 4, 6
4, 2, 5, 3, 5, 2, 4, 3, 4, 1, 3, 4, 4, 1, 5, 2, 4, 5, 3, 4

a) In the space below group together the results in a frequency table.

b) What percentage of the houses have 3 or more residents? ....

Sorting Data 1 & 2 (cont)

4 The test results for a group of students are given below.

Group the data to complete the frequency table below.

31	61	40	63	65
78	52	57	~~15~~	35
77	~~11~~	68	46	68
64	70	26	87	49

Test Mark	Tally	Frequency
0-19	II	2
20-39		
40-59		
60-79		
80-99		

5 John recorded the temperature at midday every day for the month of June.

All the temperatures are to the nearest degree Celsius.

a) Group together John's results by completing the frequency table.

Temperature (°C)	Tally	Frequency
5 ⩽ T < 10		
10 ⩽ T < 15		
15 ⩽ T < 20		
20 ⩽ T < 25		

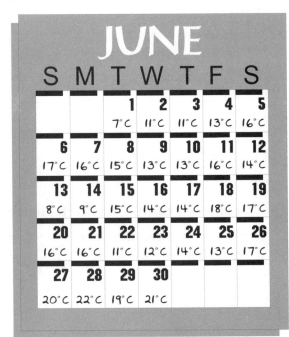

b) What percentage of the recorded midday temperatures in June are 15°C or more?

6 Bolton Wanderers scored the following number of goals in Premier League matches for the 2002/2003 season.
1, 1, 1, 1, 2, 1, 1, 0, 1, 1, 1, 1, 4, 1, 0, 1, 0, 1, 4
0, 0, 0, 1, 0, 1, 4, 1, 1, 0, 2, 1, 2, 0, 1, 0, 2, 0, 2
Group together the data in a frequency table.

7 Emma decided to measure the height (h) of all the students in her class.
Here are the results, to the nearest cm:
171, 178, 166, 173, 180, 173, 186, 176, 170, 184, 178, 174, 169, 189, 175, 182, 181, 171, 179, 164, 178, 175, 174, 191, 169, 178, 173, 188, 167, 192.

a) Sort the data into a frequency table using class intervals 160 ⩽ h < 165, 165 ⩽ h < 170 etc.
b) What percentage of the students in Emma's class have a height measurement of 170cm or more?

8 The individual weights of 40 people, to the nearest kg, are as follows:
79, 75, 68, 70, 83, 72, 81, 89, 61, 74, 80, 51, 84, 63, 73, 54, 76, 74, 80, 85, 94, 77, 71, 81, 70, 66, 87, 62, 59, 63, 63, 67, 75, 81, 80, 78, 60, 77, 61, 75.
Sort the data into a frequency table using appropriate class intervals.

1 The following data shows the age (in years) of 30 shoppers in a supermarket.

41, 51, 8, 60, 21, 31, 41, 17, 68, 28, 34, 45, 46, 52, 74, 56, 10, 23, 47, 30, 34, 9, 42, 29, 55, 44, 38, 57, 47, 58

Using tens to form the 'stem' and units to form the 'leaves', draw a stem and leaf diagram to show the data.

2 A survey of 120 people was conducted to find out if they listen to the radio whilst driving. Complete the two way table to show the results.

	Men	Women	Total
Listen to radio	32	....	73
Do not listen to radio	....	24	....
Total	55	....	....

3 A survey of 200 Year 7, 8 and 9 pupils was carried out to find their favourite type of music from a choice of three: Pop, Rap or Dance.

a) Complete the two way table to show the results.

	Year 7	Year 8	Year 9	Total
Pop	42	....	18	....
Rap	....	12	....	41
Dance	14	....	31	69
Total	....	....	62	....

b) What percentage of the pupils chose Pop as their favourite type of music?

....

4 Here are the heights, to the nearest cm, of 30 students in a class:
171, 178, 166, 173, 180, 173, 186, 176, 170, 184, 178, 174, 169, 189, 175, 182, 181, 171, 179, 164, 178, 175, 174, 191, 169, 178, 173, 188, 167, 192.
a) Using tens to form the 'stem' and units to form the 'leaves' draw a stem and leaf digram to show the data.
b) What is the modal class of the data?
c) What is the median value of the data?

Displaying Data 1

1 A survey was carried out to find the favourite type of music for a group of people. The results are displayed in this pictogram.

Country
Pop
Classical
Jazz
Rock

Where ⬤ represents four people.

Draw a bar graph to show this information.

2 36 primary school children were asked to name their favourite pet.

$\frac{1}{3}$ said DOG

$\frac{1}{4}$ said CAT

$\frac{2}{0}$ said FISH

$\frac{1}{12}$ said RABBIT

… and the remainder said BIRD.

Draw a bar graph to show this information.

3 This bar chart shows the different types of milk sold in a supermarket and the actual number of pints sold on one day.

a) What was the second most popular type of milk sold?

....

b) How many pints of milk are sold in total?

....

c) In the space below draw a pictogram to show this data:

---

4 Draw **a)** a pictogram and **b)** a bar graph to show the data recorded in question **2** on page 129.

5 Repeat for question **3** on page 129.

Displaying Data 2 & 3

1 A group of factory workers were asked how long it took them to get to work.

This table shows the results. Construct a frequency diagram to show this information.

Time, t (minutes)	Number of workers i.e. Frequency
$0 \leqslant t < 10$	21
$10 \leqslant t < 20$	14
$20 \leqslant t < 30$	28
$30 \leqslant t < 40$	8
$40 \leqslant t < 50$	4

2 In a survey 50 women were asked how much they spend on cosmetics in one week.

The results are shown in the table below.

Money Spent, M (£)	Frequency
$0 \leqslant M < 2$	1
$2 \leqslant M < 4$	6
$4 \leqslant M < 6$	28
$6 \leqslant M < 8$	11
$8 \leqslant M < 10$	4

a) Draw a frequency polygon to show the information.

b) 50 men were also asked how much they spend on cosmetics in one week. The results are shown below. On the same axes draw a frequency polygon to show the money spent by men.

Money Spent, M (£)	Frequency
$0 \leqslant M < 2$	13
$2 \leqslant M < 4$	28
$4 \leqslant M < 6$	5
$6 \leqslant M < 8$	3
$8 \leqslant M < 10$	1

c) How do the two distributions compare?

....

....

....

....

....

....

....

....

....

....

Displaying Data 2 & 3 (cont)

3 The table shows the height of a girl from birth to age 5. Her height was recorded every year on her birthday.

Height (cm)	42	51	66	75	84	89
Time (years)	0	1	2	3	4	5

a) Draw a time series to show the trend in her height.

b) Between which time period was there the greatest increase in height?

....

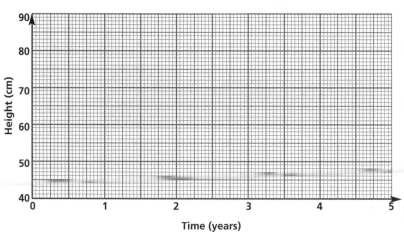

Time (years)

4 The graph below shows the sales of ice-cream at a shop at a seaside resort. What trend, if any, does the graph show?

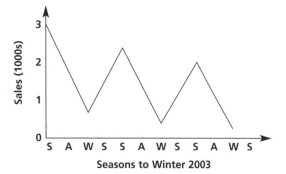

Seasons to Winter 2003

....

....

....

....

....

....

....

....

....

....

5 The table below shows the sales of shoes at a store over a six month period. Use a three point moving average to determine if there is a trend in sales.

Apr	May	Jun	Jul	Aug	Sept
103	78	83	73	57	122

....

....

....

....

....

....

....

....

6 Below are the highest recorded temperatures, in °C, on one particular day for forty places around the world.
17, 28, 33,19, 21, 28, 31, 24, 21, 20, 19, 28, 24, 19, 20, 24, 29, 32, 16, 26,
33, 24, 23, 16, 16, 20, 28, 17, 24, 23, 26, 31, 33, 18, 31, 26, 28, 19, 19, 21
a) Group together the data in a frequency table.
b) Construct a frequency diagram to show the data.
c) On separate axes construct a frequency polygon to show the data.

Histograms

1 **This table shows the distance that the workers at Barney's Biscuits have to travel to work.**

a) Complete the frequency density column in the table.

b) Draw a histogram to illustrate the data in the table.

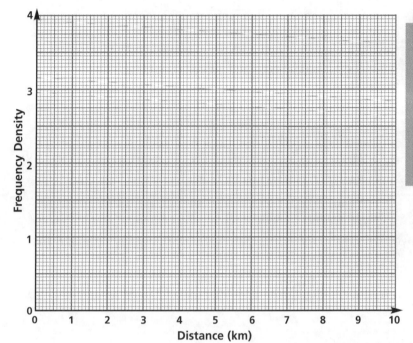

Distance (km)	Freq.	Freq. Density
0 ≤ d < 2	7	3.5
2 ≤ d < 3	3	
3 ≤ d < 4	4	
4 ≤ d < 5	2	
5 ≤ d < 10	8	

2 **This histogram shows the distribution of the number of hours that students in Kim's class spent on a coursework task. How many students are there in Kim's class?**

....

....

3 The students from Whitehall School took part in a fun run for charity. The table shows the times the students took to complete the run.

Time (min)	40 ≤ t < 60	60 ≤ t < 70	70 ≤ t < 80	80 ≤ t < 90	90 ≤ t < 100	100 ≤ t <120
Frequency	28	43	58	40	34	18

a) Work out the frequency density.

b) Draw a histogram to illustrate this data.

Scatter Diagrams 1 & 2

1 **This scatter diagram shows the average journey time and distance travelled for ten pupils travelling from home to school.**

a) What does the scatter diagram tell you about the relationship between the journey time and the distance travelled?

....

b) Draw a line of best fit.

c) Use your graph to estimate…

i) the time taken by John, who travelled a distance of 2.5 km. ....

ii) the distance travelled by Donna, who takes 27 minutes. ....

2 **The table below shows the heights and weights of 10 boys.**

Height (cm)	133	162	130	163	153
Weight (kg)	70	84	64	87	87

Height (cm)	150	124	141	150	138
Weight (kg)	77	66	79	82	69

a) Use the information given to plot a scatter diagram, including line of best fit.

b) What type of correlation is there between height and weight?

....

c) i) Tony weighs 72kg. Use your graph to estimate his height..........................

ii) Rob is 1.57m tall. Use your graph to estimate his weight. ....

3 Mrs Thrift goes shopping at her local supermarket on 12 separate occasions. Each time she pays for her items with a £10 note. The table below shows the number of items bought and change received.

Number of items bought	10	8	6	4	14	12	7	8	14	2	7	11
Change received (£)	2.50	5.60	5.70	7.80	0.90	3.10	5.20	4.20	1.50	7.90	6.80	2.70

a) Use the information given to plot a scatter diagram including line of best fit.

b) What type of correlation does the scatter diagram show? ....

....

c) i) Mrs Thrift buys 9 items. Estimate how much change she receives. ....

ii) Mrs Thrift receives £6.20 in change. Estimate how many items she bought.

....

4 The table below shows the number of tracks and total playing time for 12 music CDs.

Number of tracks	14	20	8	11	18	14
Total time (mins)	62	69	58	61	66	67

Number of tracks	10	5	16	7	18	6
Total time (mins)	56	46	66	56	69	52

a) Use the information given to plot a scatter diagram, including line of best fit.

b) i) If a CD has 13 tracks, estimate its total playing time. ....

ii) If the total playing time of a CD is 54 minutes, estimate the number of tracks it has. ....

5 The table gives information about the number of chapters and the total number of pages in books on Diane's shelf.

Number of chapters	19	28	11	14	27	23	8	16	21	25	32	19	35	11	16
Total number of pages	250	355	110	230	235	350	145	200	235	315	325	120	395	125	305

a) Use the information given to plot a scatter diagram, including line of best fit.

b) What does the scatter diagram tell you about the relationship between the number of chapters and total number of pages?

c) Use your graph to estimate **i)** the total number of pages if a book has 24 chapters,

ii) the number of chapters if a book has a total of 190 pages.

Pie Charts

1 In one week a travel agent sold 120 separate holidays.
The table below shows the holiday destinations.

Holiday Destination	No. of Holidays Sold
Spain	42
Greece	12
France	34
Cyprus	22
Italy	10

a) Draw and label a pie chart to represent these destinations.

b) What percentage of the holidays sold were for Spain?

....

c) What fraction of the holidays sold were for Greece?

....

2 Rose has completed 40 pieces of work in Maths in one school year. Her grades are as follows:

B, C, A, B, C, D, B, C, B, E, D,
A, B, C, D, B, C, B, B, D, A, C,
C, B, A, D, A, C, B, C, B, A, D,
E, C, B, C, C, B, D.

a) Draw a table to show the distribution of grades.

b) Draw and label a pie chart to show the distribution.

c) What fraction of Rose's grades were As or Bs?

....

❸ 60 men and 60 women were asked, 'What is your favourite colour of car?'
The two pie charts show the results.

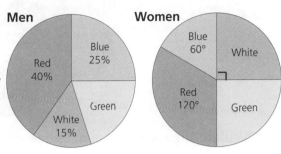

a) i) How many men chose red as their favourite colour?

....

ii) How many women chose red as their favourite colour?

....

b) Did more men or women choose green as their
favourite colour? Show your working.

....

....

❹ This pie chart shows the daily newspaper bought by 72 people.

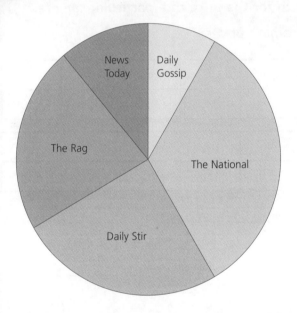

a) i) Which is the most popular newspaper? ....

ii) Which is the least popular newspaper? ....

b) i) How many people buy the Daily Stir?

....

ii) How many more people buy The National
compared to News Today?

....

....

....

....

....

❺ This table shows the number of telephone calls Mrs Chattergee makes in one week.

Day of the week	Monday	Tuesday	Wednesday	Thursday	Friday	Saturday	Sunday
Number of phone calls	3	2	8	4	7	10	6

a) Draw and label a pie chart to represent the information.
b) What percentage of the telephone calls were made at the weekend?

❻ The ages of the people living in Addick Close are as follows:
2, 24, 14, 8, 70, 15, 19, 31, 85, 4, 3, 12, 30, 27, 45, 50, 66, 68, 2, 11,
74, 31, 63, 28, 41, 47, 51, 14, 18, 83, 69, 7, 52, 35, 33, 20, 14, 6, 7, 5.
a) Construct a frequency table to show the distribution of ages using class intervals of 1-20, 21-40, etc.
b) Draw and label a pie chart to show the distribution. c) What percentage of the residents are aged 41 or more?

❼ A group of men and women were asked how they travel to work.
The two pie charts show their responses. They are not drawn accurately.
a) If 10 men travel to work by car, how many men
travel to work by i) bus? ii) train?
b) If 20 women travel to work by train, how many women
travel to work by i) car? ii) bus?

Mean, Median, Mode & Range 1

1 Laura has the following coins in her pocket:

Calculate the mean, median, mode and range for the value of the coins.

Mean: ....

....

Median: .... Mode: .... Range: ....

2 The table below shows the results of an Internet search for the price of a particular camera.

Calculate the mean, mode, median and range of the camera prices.

Camera	1	2	3	4	5	6	7	8	9	10
Cost (£)	227	246	248	248	169	204	220	165	225	210

Camera	11	12	13	14	15	16	17	18	19	20
Cost (£)	239	227	211	248	166	170	155	153	196	173

Mean: ....

....

Median: .... Mode: .... Range: ....

3 The weights of the 11 players in the Year 11 hockey team were measured.

Their weights in Kilograms were: 51, 60, 62, 47, 53, 48, 52, 51, 65, 61, 66

a) Calculate the mean, median, mode and range for their weights.

Mean: ....

....

Median: .... Mode: .... Range: ....

b) The weights of the 11 players in the Year 10 hockey team were also measured.

Their mean was 52.5kg and the range was 11kg. Compare the weights of the two teams.

....

....

4 **9A contains 14 girls. Their heights in metres are:**
1.46, 1.62, 1.57, 1.60, 1.39, 1.71, 1.53, 1.62, 1.58, 1.40, 1.46, 1.63, 1.62, 1.65
a) Calculate the mean, median, mode and range for the heights.
b) The boys in 9A have a mean height of 1.68m and a range of 0.32m. Compare the heights of the girls and the boys.

Mean, Median, Mode & Range 2 & 3

1 0Janet carries out a survey on the number of passengers in cars which pass her house.

Here are the results:

Number of passengers	Frequency	Frequency x No. of passengers
0	11	
1	12	
2	6	
3	8	
4	3	

a) How many cars were there in her survey? ....

b) What is the modal number of passengers? ....

c) What is the median number of passengers? ....

d) What is the range of the number of passengers? ....

e) What is the mean number of passengers?

....

....

....

2 This graph shows the number of chocolate bars bought by pupils at a school tuck shop.

a) How many pupils bought chocolate bars? ....

b) What is the modal number of bars bought? ....

c) What is the median number of bars bought? ....

d) What is the mean number of bars bought?

....

....

....

3 The table gives the recorded midday temperature every day for June.

a) Complete the table and work out an estimate of the mean recorded temperature.

Temperature, T (°C)	Frequency	Mid-temp values (°C)	Frequency x Mid-temp values
$5 \leqslant T < 10$	3	7.5	3 x 7.5 = 22.5
$10 \leqslant T < 15$	14	12.5	....
$15 \leqslant T < 20$	11	....	....
$20 \leqslant T < 25$	2	....	....

b) In which class interval does the median lie? ....

c) What is the modal class? ....

4 Phil carries out a survey about the amount of pocket money his classmates each receive every week. The results are shown below. Complete the table.

Amount of pocket money, M (£)	Frequency		
0 ⩽ M < 2	3		
2 ⩽ M < 4	15		
4 ⩽ M < 6	8		
6 ⩽ M < 8	5		
8 ⩽ M < 10	1		

a) Calculate an estimate of the mean amount of pocket money the pupils receive.

....

....

b) In which class interval does the median lie? ....

c) What is the modal class? ....

5 The graph shows the amount of time Narisha had to wait for a bus to take her to school each morning for half a term.

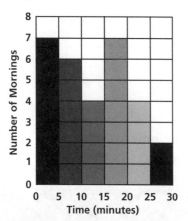

a) How many mornings are shown altogether? ....

b) Calculate an estimate of the mean amount of time Narisha had to wait for a bus.

....

....

....

....

....

6 The table below shows the number of goals scored by the Year 11 football team in one season.

Number of goals scored	0	1	2	3	4	5	6
Number of games	7	5	11	3	3	0	1

a) What is **i)** the mean **ii)** the range **iii)** the mode and **iv)** the median of the number of goals scored?
b) The Year 10 football team's mean was 2.2 goals per game in five fewer games. Which year scored the most goals and by how many?

7 During a PE lesson the boys have a 100m race. Their times were recorded and the results are shown below:

Time taken, t(seconds)	12 < t ⩽ 14	14 < t ⩽ 16	16 < t ⩽ 18	18 < t ⩽ 20	20 < t ⩽ 22	22 < t ⩽ 24
Number of boys	2	9	13	5	3	1

a) Calculate an estimate of the mean time **b)** In which class interval does the median lie? **c)** Which class interval is the mode?

Cumulative Frequency 1 & 2

1 This cumulative frequency graph shows the time taken for 30 students to complete their maths homework.

a) How many students took less than 40 minutes?

....

b) How many students took more than 40 minutes?

....

c) What was the median time taken?

....

2 Thirty five people took part in a skateboarding competition. The points they scored are shown in the table below.

Points scored (P)	Frequency	Cumulative Frequency
$0 < P \leqslant 5$	2	
$5 < P \leqslant 10$	4	
$10 < P \leqslant 15$	5	
$15 < P \leqslant 20$	7	
$20 < P \leqslant 25$	12	
$25 < P \leqslant 30$	5	

a) Complete the cumulative frequency column in the table.

b) Draw the cumulative frequency graph.

c) Use the graph to estimate…

i) The median points scored ....

ii) The inter-quartile range ....

d) How many competitors scored between 15 and 25 points?

....

e) How many competitors scored more than 25 points?

....

....

Cumulative Frequency 1 & 2 (cont)

❸ The cumulative frequency graph shows
the Resistant Materials test results for 80 boys.
The test was out of 50.

a) What was the median result?

....

b) What was the inter-quartile range?

....

c) How many boys scored more than 45?

....

d) 80 girls also completed the test. The table
below shows their results. Complete the table.

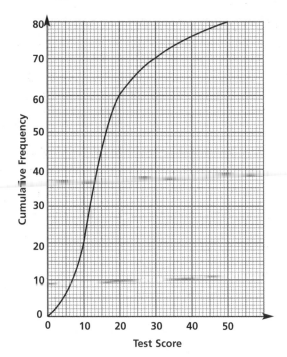

Test Result (T)	Frequency	Cumulative Frequency
0 < T ≤ 10	4	
10 < T ≤ 20	13	
20 < T ≤ 30	19	
30 < T ≤ 40	34	
40 < T ≤ 50	10	

e) Draw the cumulative frequency curve for the
girls on the same graph.

f) What was the median result for the girls?

....

g) How do the two results compare? Use two readings to support your comparisons.

....
....
....
....

❹ The heights in cm of 300 pupils were recorded as shown.
  a) Complete the table, adding a cumulative frequency column.
  b) Draw the cumulative frequency curve.
  c) Use your graph to find **i)** Median height **ii)** Inter-quartile range
    iii) Number of students taller than 155cm.

Height(h)	Frequency
130 < h ≤ 140	10
140 < h ≤ 150	39
150 < h ≤ 160	95
160 < h ≤ 170	125
170 < h ≤ 180	31

❺ In one week a doctor weighed 80 men.
The table shows the results:

Weight	50 < W ≤ 60	60 < W ≤ 70	70 < W ≤ 80	80 < W ≤ 90	90 < W ≤ 100
Frequency	11	27	29	8	5

a) Draw a cumulative frequency curve.
b) Use your graph to estimate ...
  i) Median weight **ii)** Inter-quartile range
c) What percentage of men weighed more than 70kg?